Nothing in my hand I bring

**Understanding the
differences between
Roman Catholic and
Protestant beliefs**

Ray Galea

Nothing in my Hand I Bring
© Matthias Media 2007

Matthias Media
(St Matthias Press Ltd ACN 067 558 365)
PO Box 225
Kingsford NSW 2032
Australia
Telephone: (02) 9663 1478; international: +61-2-9663-1478
Facsimile: (02) 9663 3265; international: +61-2-9663-3265
Email: info@matthiasmedia.com.au
Internet: www.matthiasmedia.com.au

Matthias Media (USA)
Telephone: 724 498 1668; international: +1-724-498-1668
Facsimile: 724 498 1658; international: +1-724-498-1658
Email: sales@matthiasmedia.com
Internet: www.matthiasmedia.com

ISBN 978 1 921068 87 4

Cover design and typesetting by Lankshear Design Pty Ltd.

Nothing in my hand I bring

Understanding the
differences between
Roman Catholic and
Protestant beliefs

Ray Galea

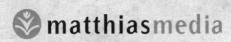 matthiasmedia

For my dear wife, Sandy, and my three patient children,
James, Amy, Madeleine.

A big thanks to Tony Payne, without whom this
book could not have been written; to my parents,
Tom and Rita, whose love is never-ending;
and to St Alban's Multicultural Bible Ministry,
whose support enabled me to write this book.

Nothing in my hand I bring,
simply to thy cross I cling;
naked, come to thee for dress;
helpless, look to thee for grace;
foul, I to the fountain fly;
wash me, Saviour, or I die.

Rock of Ages
~ AM Toplady (1740-1778)

Contents

Chapter 1
⊕ Growing up Catholic

Sᴄʜᴏᴏʟ ᴡᴀꜱ ᴏᴠᴇʀ for the day, and we were waiting for our buses outside the front gates of St Aidan's Primary School. I asked my friend, Charlie Gauci, "Which direction does your bus go to take you home?"

"My bus goes down this road and then turns right at the church that is not a Catholic church", he said.

I think that was the very first time it dawned on me that there were such things as churches that were not Catholic churches. I was eight years old. Little did I know then that thirty years later I would end up the minister of that church at the end of the road that was not a Catholic church.

I grew up in a devout Maltese Australian Roman Catholic home, which meant we went to mass three times a week—Sunday, Friday night and Tuesday Novena. To be Maltese was to be Catholic. No matter how tired my parents were at the end of the week on the farm, no matter which cousins we visited on Sunday—and there were many—we always attended mass. (It's a discipline I have since learnt to appreciate.)

Throughout my youth, my mother taught me that God was personal—not so much through formal lessons, but through everything she said and did. God-talk was always on her lips, and it left a lasting and profound impression on me. That was probably one reason I never doubted the existence of God.

Strangely, I have no memory of praying personal or conversational prayers as a family. Nevertheless, my mother diligently led us in saying the Rosary each night with no resistance from my father, who would sometimes be found with his head slumped back on the lounge chair gasping for air, fast asleep after a hard day's work, while we giggled through "Hail Mary, full of grace ..."

My memories growing up as a Roman Catholic were mostly positive. Our parish priest, Father Morreau, was so deeply loved by everyone in the community—even the Anglicans—that they named the local reserve after him. As his altar boy for eight years, I remember him patiently answering my questions: "If the Pope died while visiting Australia, would they bury him in Australia or ship his body back to Rome?" And: "Could a boy become a pope?"

I clearly had high ambitions.

I was a Catholic child and then teenager during the time of Vatican II, the Church Council that brought in some major reforms. For example, unlike my brother I have no memory of the Mass being said in Latin, as it had been for over a thousand years before. More of the Bible began to be read in the Mass, and there was a strong push to have the homily or sermon connect with the Bible readings. There were attempts to make the Mass understandable and an expression of fellowship—as seen by the introduction of the 'sign or kiss of peace' which we gave to each other (which was not to everyone's liking). Ecumenism, or unity with other denominations, had become a much talked about topic, although my parents never exhibited any prejudice toward non-Catholics. My father judged a man on his character not his creed.

However, the change that struck me most forcefully at that time was in the public face of God. The stern God of judgement and wrath became more of a God of love and peace. It was almost matched by a change in the nuns who ran my primary school. The school went from being run by the Sisters of St Joseph, with their heavy, forbidding, brown habits, to the Franciscan Missionaries of Mary, who wore a light white veil.

In the lead-up to my first holy communion, I remember being told of the fires of purgatory which, while not quite eternal, came close to images of hell itself. But as time went on, the God who was hard to please was replaced by the God who was quick to forgive. The change was typified (some years later) by a series of TV ads the Catholic Church ran, which asked the question through a catchy song: "When you get to heaven, what do you think He'll say?" The answer was "G'day!"—where once we might have been threatened with "Get out!" After Vatican II, salvation appeared to be open for all, and not just Catholics.

I clearly remember learning the doctrine of the Trinity in second class from a wonderfully kind American nun who also assured me that Australia would never win the America's

Cup. She had the Trinity right at least. Every prayer we prayed was ushered in by the self-blessing of the sign of the cross and the familiar words, "In the name of the Father and the Son and the Holy Spirit". The Trinity, which was revealed in the Bible and clarified in the fourth-century Nicene creed, confessed that Jesus was "God from God, light from light, true God from true God, begotten, not made". I've since realized that I could have been a Catholic in the fourth century.

How I pray even now has been influenced by some of the prayers found within the first section of the Mass, called 'the liturgy of the Word'. One of my favourites is the 'Gloria in Excelsis' from the fourth century:

> You alone are the Holy One,
> You alone are the Lord,
> You alone are the Most High,
> Jesus Christ,
> with the Holy Spirit,
> to the glory of God the Father.
> Amen.

It doesn't get any better than that!

As I look back on my Catholic upbringing, there are lots of fond memories. I am indebted to the foundation I received, and for deep convictions on a number of ethical matters, such as the protection of the unborn.

I understand that not all Catholics share the same fond memories. Some endured the occasional vicious nun, who cracked the ruler over the knuckle for writing left-handed; or worse, a molesting brother or priest who destroyed the lives of the vulnerable. As time would reveal, Roman Catholicism would not be the only church to bear this shame.

But I have no story to tell like this. My parents were devout in their faith, my parish priest was sincere, and the nuns who taught me were mostly kind. It was truly a loving Catholic home and a caring Catholic community.

Even so, as I grew older, it began to dawn on me that being Catholic was more about belonging than believing. For a good number of Roman Catholics, going to mass, which still remains a day of obligation, did not seem to be an obligation at all. They just didn't go. In fact, some seemed quite comfortable to write 'Roman Catholic' on the census and yet openly profess that they did not even believe in God.

Growing up Catholic, I assumed that the majority of Australians belonged to this community I belonged to. As a Maltese Catholic, I had a truckload of relatives who shared the same faith. I attended a Catholic primary and secondary school, where pretty much everyone was Catholic. In fact, it wasn't until about fifteen years ago that I realized with a shock that only about a quarter of the population identified themselves as Catholic, and the vast majority of those were not at all devout.

The result was that I saw myself belonging to what I thought was the majority, and this gave me a sense of security and confidence. It also seemed to me that Catholic Church buildings seemed larger and much better attended.

Up until my late teens, I saw no real distinction between Protestants, the Orthodox and the Jehovah's Witnesses. In my understanding, if you were not Catholic you were part of a cult and most probably a Jehovah's Witness (who, interestingly, have a high success rate among Catholics). I did love the way my mum, who never took a backward step, could out-talk and out-argue any member of the Kingdom Hall who knocked on our door.

Looking back, one of the oddest things about my Catholic upbringing was my attitude to Jesus. I may have prayed the 'Gloria in Excelsis' with its exalted view of Jesus as the supreme and only Lord, but I had no personal sense of Jesus' complete authority over *my* life, or his centrality for the Christian life.

Perhaps it had something to do with my culture's constant reference to Jesus as "the infant" (*il Bambin*), and the many statues depicting the infant Son of God in Mary's arms. I certainly revered Jesus as a model of faithful and sacrificial obedience, and as a teacher second to none, but I would hardly say that he was the focus of my spirituality. In fact, like many Catholics, I was suspicious of people who made too much of Jesus, or spoke of friendship with Jesus in personal terms. They were 'Jesus freaks' and 'Bible bashers' as far as I was concerned, and were to be avoided at all times. I was much more comfortable with Mary being spoken of in such personal terms.

Like many young people, my late teens were a time when any relationship with God was going to be on my terms. I somehow managed to get God to agree with pretty much everything I did. He was most compliant, or so I thought.

While studying Social Work at Sydney University, I got to know Anne, who came from a home that did not believe in God. To my surprise, she started becoming one of those 'Jesus freaks'. It began with her reading a Bible in her bedroom, and then deciding to surrender her life to Jesus. It did not take me long to realize that she had something I did not have. The living Jesus, and not just God, was very real in her life.

One day Anne challenged me. "Ray," she said, "Jesus is either Lord of everything, or he is a liar or a lunatic. Who do you think he is? You need to make a decision." She could have said more but she didn't need to. I realized the implications straight away. I could see that if Jesus was not my Lord, then I was in trouble. But since I was not prepared to change my lifestyle for anyone, I did what a lot of people do in those circumstances—I put the idea on the back burner and tried not to think about it.

That worked, at least for a while. A year later, in November 1980, I was living in the beach-side suburb of Bondi in a house full of travelling New Zealanders. Early one morning, I was walking near the sewerage outlet at Dover Heights when it came again to my mind that if Christianity was true and Jesus really was the Lord and the Son of God, then I was in big trouble, because I was ignoring the most important Person in the universe. I also realized that despite my Catholic upbringing and all the teaching and instruction I'd received, I had never seriously examined the claims of Christ for myself.

Fortunately, something else from my Roman Catholic youth came to mind at that point. I remembered the Bible being read at mass and Jesus saying, "Ask and it will be given to you, seek and you will find ..." I understood this to be a promise that I would not be disappointed if I genuinely searched for Jesus. So I made a pact with God based on this promise. I vowed to read the Bible, and it was up to him to persuade me if it was true, and I presumptuously asked if he could do it in three weeks. I just didn't see myself embarking on a lifelong search for enlightenment. Patience was never one of my virtues.

I began my search with the Bible for two reasons. Studying history at university taught me that if you want to get to the bottom of something, you go to the primary documents. You don't simply read what other people said later about it—you try to get back to what was actually said and done. You examine the sources that are closest to the time. And those sources were obviously the books of the New Testament. Secondly, I reasoned that whatever differences there were among Christian denominations, one thing they all agreed on was that the Bible was the word of God.

So I read the Gospels. I read them for the first time as an adult, and I had but one question as I read: "Is Jesus the eternal Son of God?" If he was, then I was prepared to surrender my life to him. If he wasn't, I could walk away knowing that I had genuinely looked at the evidence.

Reading the Gospels like this, really for the first time, was a profound experience. I knew a lot of the stories. Familiar snippets and quotations and incidents kept rising up to greet me. But what was completely new and unfamiliar to me was the portrait of Jesus that emerged as I read. I have to say that I simply fell in love with the Jesus that I met in the Gospels. There was a ring of truth about him, and about what he said and did. This was Jesus, the Son of God, in all his glory, and I couldn't deny it.

Several weeks later, I was in the Hotel Bondi with two of my friends, Peter and Vince, both Catholics. They knew I had been reading the Bible, and they were both a bit concerned that I might become one of those 'Bible-bashing Christians'.

They tried to dissuade me by listing out all the changes I would have to make if I were to become a Christian. Since we all sinned in the same areas, they knew very well the kinds of things I did, and what changes I would have to make if I decided to follow Jesus.

After twenty minutes of walking through all the changes I would have to make, the choice was pretty stark. I realized that I could keep living on my terms, doing all these things that I currently did for the next sixty years, and be cut off from God forever. Or I could surrender to Jesus as the Lord, make a completely fresh start, and enjoy forgiveness now and acceptance on the Last Day. The penny had dropped, and there and then I told Vince and Peter, "Guys, you have just persuaded me. I am a Christian." This was the decisive change in my life, but it would not be the only change.

The first decision as a Christian was to confess that Jesus was my Lord. The second decision was to start living with him as my Lord—to stop doing those things that grieved him, and to start doing things that honoured and pleased him. At the time, my friends understandably thought it was a phase that would pass, but I had the taste of truth in my mouth. That truth was a person, the Lord Jesus.

If Jesus was to be my Lord and Saviour, I needed to think through which church to go to. I did not want to assume that just because I was born a Catholic, this was by definition the right choice. I knew I could just as easily have been born a Baptist or a Mormon. So I spent the next six months reading and talking to priests and ministers to find out the differences between Catholics and Protestants. How did each of their teachings compare with the teaching of Jesus and the apostles?

To my surprise and hurt, I gradually, reluctantly and painfully discovered that every 'distinctive' teaching of Roman Catholicism seemed to undermine the person and work of the Lord Jesus. A time came when I realized that the differences were not superficial, and that I could not with a clear conscience remain a Roman Catholic. I felt I could no longer remain within the Catholic Church and be true to the Lord Jesus.

Making that decision public before my friends was one thing; telling my parents, whom I deeply loved, was another. My mum didn't mind me going to a Protestant church as well as going to mass. But to reject Catholicism must have felt to her like a personal rejection of her faith, her parenting and her community. It was a rejection of everything she held dear. And above all, it was a rejection of what she saw as the path to salvation.

My memory is that she cried every day for nearly two years because of my decision. No sin I turned away from was harder than seeing this impact on my mother. I was left clutching the words of Jesus: "Whoever loves father or mother more than me is not worthy of me, and whoever loves son or daughter more than me is not worthy of me" (Matt 10:37).

IT'S COMMON THESE DAYS to disparage searching for the truth. "What is 'truth' anyway?" people say. "It's all just a matter of opinion." It's funny, though, how passionate we get about the truth when we are misquoted or misunderstood. Or when someone lies to us and rips us off—whether it's a shop assistant or the government.

The truth really does matter. And the truth about Jesus matters most of all. Ask and it will be given to you, said Jesus. Seek and you will find. When I went searching for the truth, and found it in the person of Jesus himself, it eventually led me to the realization that the differences between Catholics and Protestants were large and significant. It led me to the unavoidable decision to leave the church I had loved growing up in.

As I write these words, the feelings well up inside me again—the pain of having hurt family members, the sense of having betrayed my culture and community, the accusations of arrogance ("What makes you think you know more than the Pope?!").

But in the end, once you are convinced that something is true, integrity demands that you stand by those convictions. I remember as a teenager being inspired by two films about men who stuck to their convictions in the face of enormous pressure. One was *Serpico*, with Al Pacino playing an honest cop who would not compromise his integrity in the midst of a corrupt New York police force. The other, somewhat ironically, was *A Man for All Seasons*—the story of how Thomas More stood up to King Henry VIII when the King rejected the Roman Catholic Church to obtain a divorce.

Both men were men of conviction. They saw that the truth mattered, and that integrity mattered, and they were prepared to pay the price for their convictions.

Whatever your own views as you come to this book, my prayer is that you will seek the truth about Jesus, and that when you find it—as God promises that you will if you honestly seek—you will grasp it and hold it tight. For as hard as the search can be, and as painful as the consequences may sometimes be, when you find the truth, as Jesus said, it sets you free.

Chapter 2
⊕ Which Catholicism?

THE ITALIAN MAGAZINE *L'Espresso* conducted an interesting experiment recently.[1] It sent reporters to 24 Catholic churches around Italy where, in the confessional, they sought rulings from the local priests on various thorny ethical dilemmas. The results showed a considerable gap between the teachings of the Church and the advice given by Roman Catholic priests.

In Naples, one of the journalists asked whether it was a sin to switch off the respirator that kept her father alive. In defiance of Catholic teaching on euthanasia, the priest replied, "I myself, if I had a father, a wife or a child who had lived for years only because of artificial means, would pull out [the plug]".

Another journalist posed as a researcher trying to decide whether to accept a job abroad working in embryonic stem cell research. The priest gave him the go ahead.

Still another priest, in spite of the Church's official

teaching on homosexual behaviour, told a practising gay man in Rome that, "Generally, the best attitude is to be yourself—what in English is called 'coming out'".

There was only one issue—abortion—where the priests all held to official church doctrine.[2]

The *L'Espresso* experiment highlights an important question that needs to be asked before we start to explore the differences between Catholicism and Protestantism. And that is: "Which Catholicism are we talking about?" On the surface, Roman Catholicism may appear to be a monochrome faith in which all Catholics believe the same core doctrines authorized by the teaching office of the Church of Rome. This unified picture is reinforced by the fact that regardless of which country you go to, the Mass is essentially the same. When you compare this to Protestant church services, which vary enormously in style and theology, the Catholic Church ends up looking like a kind of spiritual McDonald's—it's the same brand everywhere, and you know what you are going to get.

However, you only have to talk to two Catholics—even two Catholic priests—to find that they can have very different views on Catholicism and its teaching. One of the ways in which Catholicism and Protestantism are in fact quite similar these days is that they both contain a wide spectrum of beliefs and attitudes, among both clergy and laity.

Within Catholicism, the ultra-conservative or traditionalist end of the spectrum rejects some or all of the changes brought by the Second Vatican Council. Mel Gibson is a popular face of this movement that wants a return to the Council of Trent and for the Mass to be said only in Latin.[3] Some in this movement would hold that salvation is found only within Catholicism.[4]

Others would even deny that the last four popes were legitimate. Traditionalists can be found mostly within the Catholic Church, although in some cases they have left the Church (or been ejected), and now run independent churches, seminaries, schools and monastic orders.

In contrast, mainstream Catholicism essentially welcomes the changes brought by Vatican II without rejecting core traditional Catholic beliefs. There is a general respect for the authority of the Church's hierarchy but an equally strong desire for the reforming spirit of Vatican II to continue. Some of these hoped-for changes include ministerial reforms such as the ordination of female priests, and married priests, ethical reforms such as the acceptance of artificial contraception, and theological reforms that would allow greater participation by the laity in the life of the church. Probably the majority of practising Catholics sit in this area. They baptize their children in a Catholic church, send their children to a Catholic school, get married by a Catholic priest and are regular (or at least semi-regular) at mass. They are 'good Catholics', but most would have few qualms about quietly ignoring the Church's teaching on individual issues, such as artificial contraception.

Among mainstream Catholicism, there are various sub-movements or emphases. For example, there are possibly over 100 million Charismatic Catholics who are eager for the renewal of the Church through the gifts and ministry of the Holy Spirit.[5] This movement has links with the mystical tradition that has often been strong in Catholicism, with such heroes as Saint Teresa of Avila, Saint John of the Cross and Saint Therese of Lisieux.

There is another stream that is particularly passionate about devotion to Mary and saying the Rosary. For others, social justice and involvement with the poor is the highest priority, as seen in the St Vincent de Paul Society, or the extraordinary life of Mother Teresa of Calcutta.

A more extreme expression of this social justice stream is found in 'Liberation theology', which teaches that political redemption and salvation from poverty and inequality are at the heart of the true gospel. The emphasis here tends to fall on corporate or social sin rather than personal sin. More than one priest has been known to run guns for freedom fighters in South America.

With Liberation theology, we are approaching the radical or dissenting end of the Catholic spectrum. And down at this end we would also find a growing movement that is quite sceptical about many aspects of the Bible and traditional Christianity. 'Liberalism', as it is often called, is now a prominent feature of both Protestant and Catholic thought. Liberals tend towards anti-supernaturalism, and call into question such miraculous events as the virgin birth and the bodily resurrection of Christ. I remember a visitor to my church being shocked, as I preached through the book of Exodus, that I treated it as history. He had been studying at a local Catholic university where his lecturer, who was a nun, had convinced him that the Old Testament was a myth.

Needless to say, the liberal end of the Catholic spectrum often finds itself in conflict with the hierarchy of Rome, especially during the time of the last two popes.

This is one area, then, in which I have discovered that Catholicism and Protestantism are quite similar. There is a broad spectrum of belief and practice, and many different groupings with different emphases.

However, there's an aspect of Catholicism that isn't reflected among many Protestants—as far as I can see—and which has nothing to do with factions or movements or points on a spectrum. Catholicism is as much, or sometimes more, about *belonging* than *believing*. You are born a Catholic, and as I used to be told, "Once a Catholic, always a Catholic". Within many cultures, being Catholic is not so much a personal decision as a shared family value. It's just who you are. In some cases, there can be very little understanding of Catholic doctrines—even the key ones. And this is not seen as a big problem. For a great many Catholics, Catholicism has more to do with where you come from than what you believe. And so to reject or leave Catholicism is equated with rejecting your family and your culture. This is especially the case when Catholicism is the official religion of your mother country. For those who migrate, there is often a passionate desire to hold on to the culture and religion of home.

It also must be remembered that, as in many denominations, there is a high level of nominalism within the Catholic Church—that is, people who identify themselves as Catholic, and wouldn't dream of being anything else, and yet rarely attend mass (if ever), and have very little grasp of Catholic teachings.

Folk Catholicism is what is real for most Catholics. It is shaped not just by the national church or the local diocese or local priest, but by the particular subculture and family you are born into.

SO WHICH CATHOLICISM do I have in mind as I write this book?

At the basic level, it's important to understand and engage with the official and authoritative teaching of the Roman Catholic Church, which is normative and binding on all Catholics. Although there is a wide variety of views among individual Catholics the world over about all kinds of issues, the teachings of the Church itself remain very clear. They are the teachings that you would be expected to embrace if you wished to become a Catholic. And indeed, these are the teachings that I had to grapple with in deciding whether in good conscience I could remain a member of the Catholic Church.

Most of the following chapters are an examination of the core doctrinal differences between Roman Catholic teaching (as expressed by the Council of Trent and Vatican I and II) and the doctrines of historic Protestantism. Starting with the Reformation in the 16th century, Protestants have always 'protested' that certain important aspects of Roman Catholicism are incompatible with what the Bible says. My battle as a young Catholic who had surrendered his life to Christ, and wanted to follow him with integrity, was whether the Protestants were basically right. Much of what follows is a retracing of my investigation into that question.

I also need to say at this point that by 'Protestantism' I don't mean that I was comparing Catholicism with any particular Protestant denomination, such as the Anglicans, Baptists or Presbyterians—as if I was a young footballer trying to decide which club to join. Each of these Protestant denominations has its own distinctives and emphases, as well as its own human foibles and flaws. And (as in Catholicism) there is a broad range of belief and practice *within* each of them. In this book, I am simply using 'Protestant' as a convenient label for the convictions that many Bible-believing Christians have held since the time of the Reformation—namely, that the distinctive doctrines of Catholicism are seriously flawed.

We haven't the time or space to go into the history of the Reformation—but very simply, what happened was that over 450 years ago in Europe, a large number of bishops, priests, nuns and ordinary men and women decided that the Catholic Church had deviated too far from the Bible. They recognized that, over the centuries, Catholic teaching and traditions had arisen which undermined what Christ achieved. The name 'Protestant' was given to one of these groups in Germany who 'protested' against aspects of Catholic teaching, and the label soon came to refer to the whole movement. Unable to reform the Catholic Church, and in most cases not allowed to remain within it, the Protestants left to form their own churches and denominations. Many of the Protestant denominations that exist today arose from this Reformation movement in different European countries: the Presbyterian Church in Scotland, the Lutheran Church in Germany, the Church of England in England, and so on. Whatever differences they had amongst each other, they were bound together by four doctrinal truths captured in four slogans: Christ alone, the Bible alone, faith alone and grace alone.

However, I also want to acknowledge that for many everyday Catholics, these doctrinal questions aren't of pressing importance. Being Catholic, for the majority of Catholics, is much more about belonging to a community, a culture, a history, a family.

And so if you're reading this book as a Protestant, don't assume that your Catholic friend next door has even heard of some of these issues, let alone thinks they are important, or has a considered view of them. There's every chance that the official teachings of the Church with respect to Mary, or the Bible, or the sacraments, are pretty hazy in their minds.

And likewise, if you're reading this book as a Catholic, you may be in for a surprise (as I was) in discovering what your church actually teaches, and how it stacks up against the final standard in all matters of faith: the Bible.

Chapter 3
⊕ Christ and the Mass

IT WAS VERY CLEAR TO ME growing up that the Mass was the centre of Catholic devotion and worship.[1] I remember the rhythm of it. The standing and kneeling, the prayers, the songs, the bells ringing as the priest held up the bread and the wine, the quiet queues forming around the church, people shuffling forward, the smooth almost plastic taste of the wafer on your tongue, the cheery bursting out afterwards into the sunshine.

At the time, even as a young adult, I couldn't have told you exactly what was going on during the Mass. I knew that the bread was somehow the body of Christ, and that eating it was supposed to be good for my soul, but I couldn't have explained very clearly what it was all about. It was just something I did—three times a week.

If you were to read the Catechism of the Catholic Church, or ask a Catholic priest to explain the Mass, you would discover that the Mass is essentially a sacrifice. The high point is when the priest calls down the Holy Spirit on the bread and wine, turning them into the actual body and blood of Christ (that's when the bells ring). The newly present body and blood of Christ are lifted up, and worshipped and adored by the congregation as Christ himself. The priest then offers Christ as the sacrificial victim (or 'host') to God on behalf of the people. In that 'bloodless' sacrifice, God's anger is turned away and forgiveness of sins is obtained.

As a newly converted Christian trying to come to terms with Catholicism, I had to work out what I thought of the Mass. And the more I understood about the Mass, the more disturbed I became. Because I was not only reading official Catholic teachings; I was also reading my Bible. And what I read in the Bible about Christ's sacrifice didn't seem to sit too well with what was going on in the Mass.

Three areas in particular stood out as problems:

1. the role of a human priest in the place of Christ
2. the turning of bread and wine into Christ
3. the renewing of Christ's sacrifice for the forgiveness of sins.

1. The role of a human priest in the place of Christ

Without a priest there can be no mass. The bread and wine cannot change into the body and blood of Christ without a priest. The sacrifice of Christ cannot be offered without a priest. Sins cannot be forgiven without a priest.

It can be hard for non-Catholics to understand just how important the priest is for Catholic faith and life. He is in a class of his own. Unlike ordinary Christians, he is God's special instrument, possessed of supernatural power, able to "act in the person of Christ the Head".[2] Just as Christ himself is our high priest, so also the priest "is made like to the High Priest and possesses the power of performing actions in virtue of Christ's very person".[3] Priests are given the title 'Father' because "they are the means by which Christ brings life to men".[4]

What does the Bible say about all this? What do we learn in the Scriptures about priests?

The first thing we learn, via the Old Testament, is that priests are indeed a special class of people who stand between God and the rest of us. They are go-betweens, or mediators. In Old Testament Israel, a special group of men was chosen from one of the twelve tribes (Levi), and their role was to represent the rest of Israel before God at the temple. They offered sacrifices and performed the various ceremonies that God had set up so that the people could be forgiven. Within the select group of priests, one man served as high priest, and it was his privilege alone to enter into the Most Holy Place in the heart of the temple, once a year, to offer a special sacrifice of atonement for the sins of the people (see Lev 16).

However, the Old Testament style of priesthood had some major limitations. As the New Testament book of Hebrews points out, the priests themselves were fallible, sinful men, who had to make sacrifice for their own sins before they could do anything to help others, and who eventually died (as we all do as a result of sin). What's more, the sacrifices of bulls and goats that they offered didn't really deal with sin once and for all, and wipe the guilty conscience clean, as shown by the fact that they had to keep on being offered year after year. Their very repetition spoke of their ineffectiveness.

All this is argued at some length and with some complexity in Hebrews 7-10. But the main point of these chapters is very simple and stark: the Old Testament priesthood served its purpose, but it was only a shadow of what was to come. It was like a photograph; but Christ is the real thing. And now that the Real Thing has arrived, the old human priesthood is obsolete. If we now have a perfect high priest, without sin or any other imperfection, who offered one, full, completely sufficient sacrifice for sins for all time, why would we want to go back to having human priests offering sacrifices on our behalf? This was the kind of temptation the Jewish Christian readers of Hebrews faced, and the author is very clear in urging them to resist it: You don't need human priests any more; Christ has filled that role completely and perfectly forever.

You can perhaps already see why the message of Hebrews 7-10 gives me a real problem with the Roman Catholic priesthood, because Catholicism is very straightforward about the role of the human priest: "Some men are chosen by God to share the priesthood of Jesus Christ ... It is through their hands, lips and will that Christ acts to become present at Mass".[5] The human priesthood of Catholicism attempts to reinstate a kind of Old Testament-style human mediation into the process of salvation.

However, the priesthood of Christ cannot be shared by Roman Catholic priests. They have the very same problem as the Old Testament priests: they are normal, sinful human beings like the rest of us. The priest admits as much in the Mass when he prays, "Wash away my iniquity, and cleanse me from my sin". Under the new covenant, Christ alone serves as the God-appointed sinless mediator between God and man, and it is through him alone that God promises that he will remember our sins no more (Heb 8:12). As the Apostle Paul says: "[T]here is one God, and there is one mediator between God and men, the man Christ Jesus, who gave himself as a ransom for all ..." (1 Tim 2:5-6).

It is not at all surprising, then, that in the rest of the New Testament, church leaders and ministers are never called 'priests'. They are referred to as 'shepherds', 'elders', or 'overseers' and their role is to pastor the flock by teaching the word and watching over their souls, but they are not 'priests' who stand between the people and God to distribute God's grace. The Apostle Peter, for example, does not refer to himself or other church leaders as priests but as 'fellow elders': "So I exhort the *elders* among you, as a *fellow elder* ... shepherd* the flock of God that is among you, exercising *oversight*" (1 Pet 5:1-2).

It seems to me that Roman Catholicism gets all this badly wrong. By setting aside a special class of people to be 'co-priests' with Christ, they dramatically *upgrade* the status and nature of Christian ministers, and just as dramatically *downgrade* the unique and perfect priestly work of Jesus. If Christ has done everything necessary as our great high priest to wash away our sins, cleanse our consciences and bring us to God, why do we need an additional human priest to be inserted into the process—unless there is something unfinished or inadequate about Christ's priesthood? Why create a class of indispensable human priests to stand between us and Christ, when the New Testament knows nothing of the idea?

Historically, the notion of a special class of human priest who mediates between God and man arose in the fifth and sixth centuries. At that time, preaching and teaching were being under-valued in favour of ritual activity, and where there is ritual, priestly ritual-makers are usually not far behind.[6] This development reached its climax in the 12th and 13th centuries, with the formalization of the seven sacraments. The increased emphasis on the sacraments gave even more importance to the priests who administered them.

The irony of the Roman Catholic view of priests is that it misses what the New Testament actually *does* say about how Christians function as 'priests'. The New Testament draws an amazing conclusion from what Christ has done as the ultimate high priest. It says that because Christ, the great and final mediator, has dealt with sin and reconciled us to God, then all Christians now have the privileges of priests—all of us can draw near to God with confidence through the blood of Christ; every believer can approach God directly without the aid of another earthly priest in full assurance of faith (see Heb 4:16, 10:22); and thus we can all enter God's very presence and offer him 'sacrifices'—such as offering our very bodies and all that we do, as Romans 12:1-2 puts it. And just as the Old Testament priests stood between God and the people, Christians are like 'priests' in the world—we bring the news of God to people, we tell of his wonderful deeds, and we are his representatives among all nations (see 1 Pet 2:9).

At the time of the Reformation, this idea of the 'priesthood of all believers' was advanced in opposition to the Catholic view, and was condemned by the Council of Trent.[7] As Luther and others read the Bible, they saw that the people of God are not priests in the sense of offering a sacrifice that takes away sin—because that offering has already been made once and for all at the cross. However, it is the privilege of every Christian to serve God and give him pleasure through obedience. God is hard to satisfy, for nothing less than the death of Jesus did that, but he is easy to please. In Christ, a broken and contrite heart he will accept every time.

2. The turning of bread and wine into Christ

I remember my favourite nun preparing us for our first holy communion. She told us the story of the girl who decided not to swallow the consecrated host. Instead, she took it home and gently laid it in her drawer. She went out to play and came back to discover the drawer full of blood—the blood of Jesus! Stories such as these are more folk Catholicism than infallible dogma, but they capture something very important about the Catholic doctrine of the Mass: that the bread and wine truly become the body and blood of Christ himself.

Roman Catholicism teaches that the bread and wine that the priest holds in his hands at the altar is changed into the actual body and blood of Christ. Here is one of the Eucharistic prayers said by the priest alone. It is called 'the epiclesis':

> Priest: God our Father, we now ask you to send your Holy Spirit to change these gifts of bread and wine into the body and blood of Jesus Christ, our Lord.

After this prayer is said, what lies upon the altar is, despite appearances, no longer bread and wine but Christ himself. This change is called *transubstantiation* (for reasons I will explain below).

This changing of the bread and wine into the actual body of Christ is not just a theory or an idle speculation as far as Catholicism is concerned. The consecrated 'host' (as the bread is called) is given full worship and adoration in the Mass because Christ himself is present under the appearance of bread. In the feast of Corpus Christi, the host is even carried about in procession for people to adore.[8] Some of the remaining host (or 'blessed sacrament', as it is also called) is kept in a small box or 'tabernacle' in the chapel, and Catholics are encouraged to pray to it. "As they kneel or sit there before the tabernacle they realize they are in the presence of Christ Our Lord."[9]

Now it's a little difficult to explain how something can change into something else (bread into Christ) without its physical properties changing in any way. And to do this, Catholicism relies on a philosophical distinction first proposed by the Greek philosopher, Aristotle. Aristotle taught that objects in the world have two aspects to them: their surface physical properties (the bits you can see, smell, taste and touch), as well as an underlying essential quality that defines what they really are. So although all the horses in the world, for example, have different shapes, colours, sizes and other characteristics, there's a certain 'horsiness' that they all share that isn't connected to any particular surface property. Aristotle called the surface properties the 'accidents' of an object, and the underlying essential quality of something he called the 'substance'.

What happens in the Mass, according to official Catholic teaching, is that while the 'accidents' of the bread and wine remain unchanged, the 'substance' of the bread (the underlying 'breadiness' of the bread) is changed into the substance of the body and blood of Christ. There is a transformation of 'substance'—hence 'transubstantiation'.

So while the bread continues to look like bread, smell like bread, feel like bread and taste like bread—in fact, while it continues to be made up physically of nothing but bread—somehow it has been so completely transformed into the body of Christ that I am called upon to fall on my knees and worship it.

As a young person in the Catholic Church, I took it on faith that the bread and wine changed into the body and blood of Christ. I didn't understand the finer points of transubstantiation but that didn't bother me.

In fact, when i came to investigate transubstantiation and understood more about what it meant, it wasn't the illogical—or some might even say fanciful—nature of the doctrine that really disturbed me. What began to grieve me was the realization that god hated idolatry, and that this is what the mass had become.

The mass turns the eternal Son of God into an object to be worshipped and in so doing violates the second commandment.[10] One of God's great griefs in the Bible is the way that his people keep representing him by impersonal objects of worship:

> "Listen to me, O house of Jacob,
>> all the remnant of the house of Israel,
> who have been borne by me from before your birth,
>> carried from the womb;
> even to your old age I am he,
>> and to gray hairs I will carry you.

I have made, and I will bear;
    I will carry and will save.

"To whom will you liken me and make me equal,
    and compare me, that we may be alike?
Those who lavish gold from the purse,
    and weigh out silver in the scales,
hire a goldsmith, and he makes it into a god;
    then they fall down and worship!
They lift it to their shoulders, they carry it,
    they set it in its place, and it stands there;
    it cannot move from its place.
If one cries to it, it does not answer
    or save him from his trouble." (Isa 46:3-7)

The talking, seeing, listening and living God simply does not allow inanimate objects to represent him.[11] Nowhere is that clearer than in Psalm 115:

Our God is in the heavens;
    he does all that he pleases.

Their idols are silver and gold,
    the work of human hands.
They have mouths, but do not speak;
    eyes, but do not see.
They have ears, but do not hear;
    noses, but do not smell.
They have hands, but do not feel;
    feet, but do not walk;
    and they do not make a sound in their throat.
Those who make them become like them;
    so do all who trust in them.

O Israel, trust in the LORD!
    He is their help and their shield. (Ps 115:3-9)

To claim that a piece of unleavened bread is the second person of the Trinity is profoundly disrespectful. The critique of Psalm 115 applies to the deaf and dumb host that needs to be carried, elevated and worshipped.[12]

Transubstantiation is not even an argument that the Catholic Church has always accepted. As a theory to explain what was happening in the Mass, transubstantiation was first put forward by Paschasius Radbertus in the ninth century.[13] After several centuries of debate, it was finally declared to be official church dogma by the Lateran Council of 1215. Significantly, the renowned Catholic theologian Duns Scotus acknowledged in the 13th century that before this Lateran Council, transubstantiation was not an article of faith. The Council of Trent ruled that a failure to accept transubstantiation invoked an anathema or curse.

Transubstantiation seems illogical, but is it biblical? There are some parts of the Bible which, at least on face value, appear to take you in the direction of some sort of real presence of Christ in the Lord's Supper. "Take, eat; this is my body", says Jesus in the Gospels. "This cup is the new covenant in my blood" quotes Paul in 1 Corinthians 11:25. And most striking of all, Jesus says the following in John 6:53-54:

> "Truly, truly, I say to you, unless you eat the flesh of the
> Son of Man and drink his blood, you have no life in you.
> Whoever feeds on my flesh and drinks my blood has
> eternal life, and I will raise him up on the last day."

The first thing to recognize straight away is that no-one takes Jesus' words at the Lord's Supper literally, not even the Catholic church. A truly literal reading would have required the apostles to cannibalize Jesus and literally eat his flesh on the spot. Equally, a flatly literal reading of John 6 would require the Church to deny salvation to anyone who did not attend mass, because only those who eat Christ can have eternal life. This the Catholic Church is unwilling to do.

What did Jesus mean when he described the bread as his body, and the wine as his blood?

Jesus often used figurative language about himself. He called himself the door, the vine, the light, the gate and the good shepherd, to name but some. Reading the passages in their context, it seems fairly obvious that this is what he is doing at the Last Supper. When Jesus says, "This is my body, which is given for you. Do this in remembrance of me" (Luke 22:19), which of the following two options do you think he is likely to have meant?

This bread which I am holding in my hand symbolizes my body, which is about to be broken and crucified for your salvation. Whenever you eat this meal again in the future, remember what I did for you when my body was broken, and be strengthened in your faith.

Or:

This bread which I am holding in my hand looks like bread, but has in fact been mysteriously transformed into my actual flesh. Whenever you eat this meal in the future, you will actually be eating my very body in a renewing of my sacrifice.

Certainly the great Augustine of Hippo was in no doubt. Commenting on Jesus' instruction to 'eat his flesh' in John 6, he writes, "It is a figure, therefore, teaching us that we partake of the benefits of the Lord's passion and that we must sweetly and profitably treasure up in our memories that his flesh was crucified and wounded for us."

There are other objections I could raise to the doctrine of transubstantiation—such as how it ignores Jesus' bodily ascension into heaven—but space here is limited. I'll conclude instead with the testimony of Andrew Hewet, a 24-year-old tailor's apprentice, who went on trial in England in the 16th century for denying that the consecrated host was the actual body of Christ. John Foxe records this exchange between Hewet and the bishops who were trying him:

> "Do you believe it is really the body of Christ, born of the Virgin Mary?" his accusers insisted.
> "No."
> "Why not?"
> "Because", Hewet replied, "Christ commanded me not to believe all men who say, 'Behold, here is Christ, and there is Christ, for many false prophets shall arise'."
> Then the bishops smiled at him, and the Bishop of London said, "Unless you revoke your opinion, you will burn."
> "Good", said Hewet.[14]

On 4 July 1533, Andrew Hewet was burnt to death.

He wasn't the only one. At the time of the Reformation, 'transubstantiation' was one of major battlegrounds between the Catholic Church and the Reformers. The Reformers rightly saw that the doctrine of the Mass was not only idolatrous and unscriptural, but that it cut across the unique and finished work of Christ on the cross. One of their slogans was 'Christ alone'—not Christ plus the work of the priest in the Mass.

3. The renewing of Christ's sacrifice for the forgiveness of sins

Even though I was an altar boy for eight years, I never quite understood at the time that the Mass is not simply a sacrament but a sacrifice. In fact, somewhat ironically given the views I would later hold, I focused on the words "Do this in remembrance of me" as a guiding principle. I thought we were mainly remembering.

But the Mass is not a remembrance, nor even an act of 'thanksgiving' (which is what the word 'Eucharist' means). It's a sacrifice. At the heart of the Mass, Christ is offered by the priest, on behalf of his people, to God the Father. That's why the consecrated bread is called 'the host'—it comes from the Latin word *hostia*, meaning victim. During the Mass, a victim is offered in sacrifice to God, as seen in the following prayer:

> *Priest*: Pray, my brothers and sisters, that our sacrifice may be acceptable to God, the almighty Father.
>
> **All: May the Lord accept the sacrifice at your hands,**
> **for the praise and glory of his name,**
> **for our good, and the good of all his Church.**

The reason Christ is offered and offers himself in the Mass is simple. It's to atone for sins. As the Council of Trent explains: "[T]he Mass may properly be offered ... for the sins, punishments, satisfaction, and other necessities of the faithful on earth, as well as for those who have died in Christ and are not yet wholly cleansed".[15] In other words, the benefits of the sacrifice reach even to those who have died and are in purgatory.[16]

Roman Catholicism stresses that "the mass is the same

sacrifice as that of the cross, because in both we have the same victim and the same offerer ... For the same Christ, who once offered himself a bleeding victim to his heavenly Father on the cross, continues to offer himself in an unbloody manner, by the hands of his priests on our altars."[17]

In other words, the Mass blends the Lord's Supper and the cross together. One is a continuation of, or constant renewing of, the other.[18] For example, Pope Pius XII in his encyclical *Mediator Dei* reaffirmed that in the sacrifice of the Mass "the High Priest *does* what He had already *done* on the Cross, offering Himself to the Eternal Father as a most acceptable victim."[19] The Catholic Church formally denies that the Mass repeats the 'once for all' sacrifice of the cross. Rather it is a 'renewing' or 'making present' of the same eternal offering which in essence occurs outside of time and space. The Catholic Enquiry Centre puts it this way: "the Mass is not a separate Sacrifice from that of Calvary; it is the same sacrificial offering to God now made present to us who participate in it".[20]

However, it is very hard to see how something can be continually renewed if it was finally and definitively finished in space and time. And the New Testament is in no doubt about this—the sacrifice of Christ on the cross for our sins happened once for all, at a particular time and place in human history. The work of atonement is not ongoing. It is done and completed. And its benefits are only received by *faith*, not by participating in a sacramental ritual.

The book of Hebrews makes this point very clearly in contrasting Jesus' sacrifice with the repeated, ongoing sacrifices of the Old Testament priests:

And every priest stands daily at his service, offering repeatedly the same sacrifices, which can never take away sins. But when Christ had offered for all time a single sacrifice for sins, he sat down at the right hand of God, waiting from that time until his enemies should be made a footstool for his feet. For by a single offering he has perfected for all time those who are being sanctified.

And the Holy Spirit also bears witness to us; for after saying,

> "This is the covenant that I will make with them
>> after those days, declares the Lord:
> I will put my laws on their hearts,
>> and write them on their minds,"

then he adds,

> "I will remember their sins and their lawless deeds no more."

Where there is forgiveness of these, there is no longer any offering for sin. (Heb 10:11-18)

In fulfilment of the promises of old, God sent his Son to make the one, perfect, final sacrifice for the forgiveness of sins. He made the sacrifice, and then he "sat down" at God's right hand. It is a stunning image of a job completed. And once that sacrifice has been made, there can be no other. As Jesus himself said on the cross, "It is finished" (John 19:30).

The apostles Peter and Paul both say the same thing:

> For Christ also suffered once for sins, the righteous for the unrighteous, that he might bring us to God ... (1 Pet 3:18)

> For the death he died he died to sin, once for all, but the life he lives he lives to God. (Rom 6:10)

The New Testament says that Jesus is our one, perfect high priest and mediator, who has made the one, final, perfect and sufficient sacrifice for sins, and who continues to act as a mediator on our behalf before the Father:

> The former priests were many in number, because they were prevented by death from continuing in office, but he holds his priesthood permanently, because he continues forever. Consequently, he is able to save to the uttermost those who draw near to God through him, since he always lives to make intercession for them. (Heb 7:23-25)

> My little children, I am writing these things to you so that you may not sin. But if anyone does sin, we have an advocate with the Father, Jesus Christ the righteous. He is the propitiation for our sins, and not for ours only but also for the sins of the whole world. (1 John 2:1-2)

The more I investigated all this, the more puzzled and disturbed I became. The New Testament picture was so clear and unequivocal. Why cloud the issue? Why insert human priests back into the equation as 'co-priests' with Christ? Why construct a bizarre doctrine like transubstantiation so as to bring Christ's body, which is ascended into heaven, back to earth to be re-offered to the Father? Why continually renew and re-offer the body of Christ in sacrifice at the hands of human priests in order to provide atonement and cleansing for those who participate in the Mass? Does God need a weekly reminder of Christ's once-for-all death? Or are we the ones who need the reminder?

The more I thought about it, the more it seemed that Roman Catholicism kept wanting to want to find a place for human participation in the work of redemption—in articular, the participation of the Catholic Church and its priests. It was not content to watch from afar as Christ died for the ungodly, for his enemies, for sinners who were his enemies (Rom 5:6-10). It said with one breath that the sacrifice of Christ was 'once for all', but in the next breath wanted to insist that the sacrifice of Christ was only available and effective if the Church and its priests played their indispensable part in re-offering it.

I understood that impulse to find a place for my own contribution, because I have felt it. It is profoundly humbling, humiliating even, to stand before the cross of Christ and be forced to admit: "There is nothing I can say, nothing I can do, nothing I can put forward in my own defense. All I have in my hand to offer are my sins. Oh God, please forgive me."

The strange thing is, though, that this moment of base humility at the cross is also the moment of great joy. When you realize that your salvation is accomplished not by anything that you or any other human can do or contribute, but only through Christ's infinitely worthy sacrifice, made once for all, there is peace and assurance and comfort like no other. The weight of a lifetime's sin falls from your shoulders and lands at the foot of the cross, and you realize that Jesus meant what he said: "It is finished."

There is an old line about the difference between religion and Christianity that I have always loved: religion is spelt 'do'; Christianity is spelt 'done'. He done it! It may be bad English, but it's great theology.

Chapter 4
⊕ The Bible and the Church

In GRAPPLING WITH the Catholic teaching about the Mass and how it stacked up against the Bible, I came to some fairly clear, if rather disturbing, conclusions. If I was reading the Bible correctly, then it was hard to see how the Catholic Church's teaching about the Mass could be right.

"But there's your problem right there", my Catholic friends were quick to point out. "How do you know you're reading the Bible correctly? Isn't it open to various interpretations? Surely someone has to settle the argument in the end and say with authority which interpretation of the Bible is the final one. And surely that 'Someone' is the Church. It's been around since the beginning, and has the authority of the apostles."

In other words, I didn't get very far in my investigation of Catholicism before realizing that I would have to deal with some very important questions about authority: "Is the Bible the only place where God has promised to speak?" "What authority should I rely on to determine whether something is from God?" "What or who should be allowed to bind my conscience in matters of salvation and morality?"

Sources of revelation

Like Protestantism, Roman Catholicism teaches that God reveals himself in a general way through the things he has made, showing that he is divine and powerful ('general revelation'). Like Protestantism, Catholicism says that this general revelation only gets you so far, and that a special revelation from God is also necessary to show us the way of salvation. This special revelation is found in God's written word, the Bible.

However, under the 'special revelation' category, Catholicism goes one step further. The Catholic Catechism notes that God's revelation is contained not in the Bible alone but also "in the unwritten traditions, which have been received by the apostles from the mouth of Christ himself, or from the apostles themselves ... transmitted as it were, from hand to hand".[1]

So for Catholics there are two places where special information about God can be found: the Bible and the traditions of the Church. This is why Catholicism holds some doctrines to be true that aren't mentioned in the Bible. In 1854, for example, the Catholic Church declared that Mary the mother of Jesus was not born with original sin and that she lived a life free from sin. This dogma, called 'The Immaculate Conception of Mary', has no basis in Scripture whatsoever, but it is held to be an article of faith because it is held to be one of the traditions of the church.

If there are two sources of special revelation in Catholicism, there remains only one authority: the Church of Rome itself. The Church of Rome claims the God-given authority to determine how to interpret the Bible and which traditions are truly apostolic and how they should be understood.

The Catechism states: "The task of giving an authentic interpretation of the Word of God, whether in its written form or in the form of Tradition, has been entrusted to the living teaching office of the Church alone ... This means that the task of interpretation has been entrusted to the bishops in communion with the successor of Peter, the Bishop of Rome."[2]

Every genuine Christian, then, who wants to submit to Christ and learn God's will, must submit to the teaching of the Church of Rome. This is especially true when the teaching office of the church (the Magisterium) pronounces a 'dogma'.[3] The nature of a dogma is such that even if I am firmly convinced, for example, that the Immaculate Conception of Mary contradicts the Bible's teaching, I am not free to reject it. I must submit to the authority of the Church of Rome or else be in sin, even if its teaching has no biblical support, or is even against an aspect of the Bible's teaching.[4] It's a perfect circle—the Church determines what is to be believed; and if a particular dogma is challenged on biblical grounds, the Church can simply say, "We are the final and authoritative interpreters of the Bible, and we say that you're interpreting it wrongly".

The Church of Rome as the body of Christ

Needless to say, the Roman Catholic Church has a very high view of its own role in determining what Christians should believe and do. In fact, the Roman Catholic Church sees itself as the literal body of Christ; as an extension or continuation of the ministry of Jesus of Nazareth, a kind of 'permanent incarnation'. Cardinal Bellarmine spoke of Christ as sustaining and living in the Church in such a way "that she may be said to be 'another Christ'".[5]

It is on this basis that the Roman Catholic Church claims infallibility and that its teachings are without error.[6] The logic is simple: if Jesus Christ is infallible, so is his body, the Church. To listen to Christ and to listen to the Church are one and the same. It must be stressed that when we refer to the 'Church' as infallible we are specifically referring to the teaching office of the Church, not to every priest or Catholic teacher. Vatican II affirms that "The infallibility promised to the Church resides also in the body of Bishops, when that body exercises supreme teaching authority with the successor of Peter. To the resultant definition the assent of the Church can never be wanting ..."[7]

As a result of this infallible teaching office, the Catholic Church claims to be doctrinally and structurally unreformable. Whatever it has declared to be true is true infallibly, and remains true. The content of Catholic dogma can no more be reformed than the Bible.[8]

Even though there have been many observable changes within Roman Catholicism since Vatican II, and many new currents of thought, it needs to be stressed that none of the core doctrines or structures of the Church have changed.

In fact, in speaking to the Vatican II Council, Pope Paul VI warned that "The reform cannot concern either the essential conception of the Church or its basic structure."

The Catholic Church has so emphasized the unity between Christ and the Church that they have failed to understand the profound differences—the most significant one being that the body *submits* to the head (see Eph 5:23-24, for example). If the body is unreformable—if whatever it pronounces is infallibly true—then it cannot be led and taught by its head. It effectively closes its ears to the possibility of being rebuked, corrected or taught by Christ himself.

In practice, this means that the Catholic Church cannot allow the Bible to speak to or critique its core structural and theological doctrines because these are viewed as God-given and therefore off limits. These doctrines may be refined as they were in Vatican II—and sometimes 'refined' to a very significant extent—but they can never be discarded or fundamentally altered. The Church herself becomes the standard of truth and there is no authority to which she must submit and by which she must be judged.

Sometimes in discussions about these ideas, there is heated debate about the 'infallibility of the Pope'. I don't intend to spend much time on the issue, however, because it is really a subset of the bigger question of the Church's authority. The Pope is the figurehead and focus of the Church's teaching authority, and claims the authority to speak infallibly and definitively for all Christians.[9]

But does the Catholic Church, and its head the Pope, have this authority? And do the traditions of the Church have equal authority in revelation with the Bible?

The word of God and the traditions of men

In Jesus' debates with the scribes and Pharisees, the subject of religious traditions often came up. In fact, the Pharisees were constantly outraged that Jesus did not observe all the traditions that they thought were mandatory and binding on all Jews. In Matthew 15, Jesus gives perhaps his clearest teaching about the nature of traditions:

> Then Pharisees and scribes came to Jesus from Jerusalem and said, "Why do your disciples break the tradition of the elders? For they do not wash their hands when they eat." He answered them, "And why do you break the commandment of God for the sake of your tradition? For God commanded, 'Honor your father and your mother,' and, 'Whoever reviles father or mother must surely die.' But you say, 'If anyone tells his father or his mother, What you would have gained from me is given to God, he need not honor his father.' So for the sake of your tradition you have made void the word of God. You hypocrites! Well did Isaiah prophesy of you, when he said:
>
> "'This people honors me with their lips,
> but their heart is far from me;
> in vain do they worship me,
> teaching as doctrines the commandments of men.'"
> (Matt 15:1-9)

Jesus zeroes in on the problem with traditions. They have the awful potential to undermine, over time, the very obedience to God's word that they originally may have been intended to express. In this instance, the tradition of designating part of your wealth as 'given to God' (even if you still possessed it) was being used to avoid the scriptural obligation to honour and care for your parents.

Religious traditions have always been like this. Jesus quotes Isaiah to show that Israel had a long history of this problem: "in vain do they worship me, teaching as doctrines the commandments of men" (Matt 15:9). The human heart has an almost limitless capacity to get it wrong in this area; to come up with rules and regulations that may even have been quite good and useful at the start, but which gradually become distorted or corrupt, and draw people *away* from genuine obedience to God's word.

This issue was in fact one of the sparks that ignited the Protestant Reformation in the 16th century. When Martin Luther nailed his 95 theses to the door of Wittenberg Cathedral in 1517, his chief objection was to the Catholic tradition of 'indulgences'. An 'indulgence' was like a 'get out of jail free card' that could be purchased (with money) from the Church to diminish the amount of time and suffering that someone would have to undergo in purgatory.[10] This not only led to notorious financial corruption, with travelling indulgence sellers raising money for the Church, and taking a cut for themselves; it was also a travesty of God's way of salvation, won for us through Christ's death alone. Luther saw very clearly that this tradition was not only absent from the Bible, but grossly subverted what the Bible taught about getting right with God and receiving eternal life.

However, because the granting and selling of indulgences was authorized and endorsed by the infallible teaching office of the Catholic Church, Luther's criticisms fell on deaf ears. The doctrine and practice of indulgences could not be revoked—indeed, it remains in force to this day.[11] It was true and godly by definition, because the Catholic Church had declared it to be so. And if Luther saw something different in the Bible, he was wrong, because the teaching office of the Church had infallibly declared that there was nothing in the Bible to contradict indulgences.

It was a classic case of tradition trumping Scripture, as it has always tended to do, ever since the time of Isaiah and Jesus. When Scripture is no longer allowed to rule over tradition and to critique it, the teachings and traditions of men seem always to win out. The famous Catholic theologian Hans Kung got into a degree of trouble for admitting as much when he said, "tradition gets the better of Scripture, and the teaching office in turn gets the better of tradition, because it decided what the tradition is and hence also what Scripture is".[12]

It was because of this that the Protestant Reformers had as one of their catchcries 'Sola Scriptura'—the Bible alone. What they meant by this was not that the Bible was the only book that a Christian would ever read or be helped by, or that the traditions and teachings of other Christians over the centuries weren't helpful or important. What they insisted upon was that there was one final authority that ruled over all others, that critiqued all others; one throne before which all human teachings and traditions would have to kneel and be judged. And that throne was Christ himself, speaking through his word, the Bible. As Luther put it, when called upon to renounce his criticism of indulgences, and submit to the teaching of the pope: "Unless I am convicted by Scripture and plain reason—I do not accept the authority of popes and councils, for they have contradicted each other—my conscience is captive to the Word of God. I cannot and will not recant anything."

This was a key principle of the Protestant Reformation, and remains one of the most striking differences between Protestants and Catholics: that the final authority in all matters of faith and morals is found *only* in the written word of God. Other authorities and sources of knowledge will have their place—such as our reasoning, our experience of the world, and the traditions and teachings of other Christians. But the final and overruling authority belongs to God, as he speaks to us through the Scriptures.

The Protestant Reformers also saw that if the Bible is God's own inspired word, and the supreme authority, then two other things are also true about the Scriptures. Firstly, the Scriptures are *sufficient*—that is, the Bible contains all we need to be saved and to live a godly life. In the words of Paul:

> ... from childhood you have been acquainted with the sacred writings, which are able to make you wise for salvation through faith in Christ Jesus. All Scripture is breathed out by God and profitable for teaching, for reproof, for correction, and for training in righteousness, that the man of God may be competent, equipped for every good work. (2 Tim 3:15-17)

Roman Catholicism accepts that the Bible has authority, but claims that it is not sufficient—that God had additional authoritative revelation to pass on, and that this came through the oral, unwritten traditions passed down and authorized through the Catholic Church. But it is these very traditions, which are given equal status with Scripture, that eventually overwhelm Scripture and take its place—as with indulgences.

Secondly, the Reformers wanted to insist on the *clarity* of Scripture. For them, the Bible was not an impossibly mysterious volume that could only be safely interpreted by the experts in Rome. Its message of salvation was very clear, and available to be understood by anyone who approached the text with a humble, God-fearing heart. Even from childhood, Timothy had known the Scriptures that are "able to make you wise for salvation through Jesus Christ". God had not revealed himself in his word, only then to hide himself by the impossible complexity of that very same revelation. His word was clear.

In arguing for the clarity of Scripture, the Protestant Reformers didn't pretend that every part of Scripture is equally clear—some parts of the Bible are obviously more difficult to understand than others. Nor did they suggest that we should read the Bible in glorious isolation, ignoring the wisdom and insights of other Christians, including the great saints of the past.

ONE OF THE KEY DIFFERENCES between the Protestant and Catholic positions is—again—the place of the church. Once again, the Catholic Church seems to want to find a place for itself, for a human contribution, in the way God revealed himself.

If Christ alone was the mediator, the great high priest and perfect sacrifice, then why insert human priests into the process, re-sacrificing Christ in the Mass? It only clouds the issue, and in the end takes the focus off Christ and on to the priests and their ritual activity.

Likewise, if God had spoken authoritatively, finally and

clearly in the Scriptures, why insert the Church into the process, giving it power to authorize teachings and traditions alongside Scripture, and claiming for itself the supreme authority to interpret Scripture for everyone else? Again, it only clouds the issue, and in the end takes the focus off the Bible's teaching and on to the Church's teaching and traditions.

If the Church is pictured as a ship and the ocean is the world with all its religious traditions, it only takes a small crack in the hull to allow the religious traditions to seep in. The significance is not seen at first, but eventually by the time of the Reformation in the 16th century, the ship was sinking under the weight of man-made traditions.

The Reformers, like Martin Luther, didn't want to leave the Catholic Church. They wanted to repair the hull, and pump out the water. In the end, that path was not open to them, and with reluctance they left the ship. They did so not out of pride, nor over some obscure theological argument, but because (as we'll see in our next chapter) what was at issue was salvation itself.

Chapter 5
⊕ The way of salvation

PICTURE THE DAY WHEN we will all stand before our Maker —the 'Day of the Lord' as the Bible calls it, or Judgement Day. On that day, when our turn comes, God will either welcome us into his eternal kingdom or consign us to the outer darkness. We will be saved or damned.

Upon this, nearly all Christians everywhere agree, including Catholics and Protestants.

But here is the big question—some might say the biggest of all questions: Upon what basis will God judge us on that day? To put it a little crudely: How will he decide whether I am in or out? What is the way of salvation?

Protestant theology and Catholicism give very different answers to this most basic of questions. In the language of the Bible, they have different views about 'justification'—how it is that sinful people like us could ever be declared 'just' or 'righteous', and so be worthy of God's eternal kingdom.

Put simply, the Catholic view is that justification is a *process*, beginning with baptism and continuing throughout our lives, by which God acts to forgive us and then with our cooperation change us by his Spirit to become more righteous and acceptable to himself.[1] He *makes* us righteous, infusing justice and righteousness into us over time, with our own efforts and good works, and the sacraments of the church, playing key roles in how this happens. Thus, when we arrive at Judgement Day, the basis upon which God will judge us is in part what Christ did on our behalf to take away our sins, but also whether we have become sufficiently righteous in our own character to be worthy of salvation.

By contrast, Protestants point to what the Bible says very clearly in numerous places about justification—that justification is an *event not a process*. It's a once-off declaration by God that the sinner is cleared of all guilt, and is thus completely blameless and righteous in his sight because of—and only because of—the sacrifice of Christ on his behalf. According to the Bible, when God justifies us, he doesn't do it gradually by infusing righteousness into us; he *declares* us righteous when we put our faith in Christ.

Justification, then, refers to what God does *for* us once and for all, not what he does *in* us gradually over time—although what he does in us is still important. When we become Christians, God fills us with his Spirit, and works in us to produce the fruit of godliness in our lives. This is Christian growth, or what is often referred to as 'sanctification'—but it is not justification. We constantly remain justified or 'right with God' throughout our Christian walk, regardless of how we happen to be going at the time. It's a bit like being married—

some days I'm a great husband, and some days I'm not, but I am not more 'married' on some days than on others. I am always married because of the complete change in relationship and status that happened at the beginning, at the wedding.

Our only part in justification is to gladly trust (to put our 'faith') in God's offer of free forgiveness and justification. The good works that we do come *after* our justification, as a glad response to what God has already done for us.[2] As I said at the funeral of a dear lady in my church who died in Christ, "Her whole life was littered with good works, but she never trusted one of them for the forgiveness of her sins".

Is this an important difference?

Now at one level when we put the two views side-by-side like that we can see that there *is* a difference, and that it looks like a fairly significant one. Certainly, at the time of the Reformation everyone thought it was pretty significant. This was one of the key issues that drove Martin Luther and the rest of the Reformers away from Rome; and for its part, the Catholic Church was adamant that the Protestant view was completely unacceptable.

However, it is also easy to look at these two views of salvation today and think, "Does it really matter all that much? Both views have a place for faith; both have a place for doing good works; both see God at work in there somehow. Surely it's time we got past these 500-year-old theoretical arguments about theology."

This is an understandable reaction, but in the end it fails to understand how important theology or doctrine can be.

Theology is like the captain of an ocean liner. It gives us our bearings and steers us in a certain direction, and even a small change in course can result in a very different destination. Turning the wheel of the ship just a few degrees to starboard at the beginning of the journey may not seem like a big change, but it will be the difference between arriving in England or Spain by the end of the journey.

The Protestant and Catholic views of justification and salvation result in two very different kinds of Christian life, and indeed two very different churches. There are massive implications. One of them is assurance. For the Roman Catholic, there can never be any assurance of salvation, because the final verdict hinges on how well the believer has cooperated with God's Spirit through the sacraments of the Church. In fact, for Roman Catholicism it is arrogant and presumptuous to be sure of your salvation.

This came home to me when I was invited once to speak to a class of 13-year-olds at a Catholic school about the differences between Roman Catholicism and Protestant Christianity.

I opened with two questions. My first question was: "How many of you are certain that if you died tonight you would go to heaven?" Not one child put up their hand.

I then asked: "If you were to die tonight, and stand before Jesus and he were to say to you, 'Why should I let you into my kingdom?', what would you say?" I got them to write down their answers for the sake of anonymity.

Some wrote "I don't know" or "No reason why he should let me in". The majority, however, appealed to their good works in some form or other: "I've tried hard all my life to be a good person", "I was good on earth", or "I've gone to church every week and I try to be the best Catholic I can". Not one child mentioned that their hope or trust was in Christ's death for their sins. They all appealed to their good works to save them—which is the very thing that the Bible rejects.

Now I'm not suggesting that each of these kids had a perfect grasp of Catholic theology, or that they were expressing the Catholic view of salvation accurately in all its nuances. But this was their view of salvation, having been taught for many years at a Catholic school. At the same age, my answers would have been no different. Nearly every Catholic I know would say something similar. It's where the Roman Catholic ship ends up, given the direction charted by the Church. It ends up with no assurance possible that you are actually going to be saved, and a reliance on your efforts and good works to get you over the line.

The Catholic view of salvation has other massive implications as well, to do with the sacraments, and the doctrine of purgatory, to name but some. But before we discuss these, we need to explore what the Bible says on the subject. When the Reformers, like Martin Luther, objected to the Catholic Church's teaching about justification and salvation, it was because they had read the Bible and found something different there. Possibly the biblical book that affected them more than any other was Paul's letter to the Romans, because Romans deals with almost precisely the issue that the Protestant Reformers were grappling with.

Romans and justification

In Romans, Paul explains and defends a number of aspects of the gospel that he preaches, in the face of some challenges and opposition. One of the key challenges he was facing was from Jewish people who wanted to insist that whatever place Christ may have in salvation, doing the 'works of the law' was still absolutely necessary for someone to be justified before God.

Paul argues with some vigour that it is impossible for anyone to be justified before God on the basis of 'works of the law'. None of us is good enough: "[A]ll have sinned and fall short of the glory of God", he says, "and are justified by his grace as a gift, through the redemption that is in Christ Jesus, whom God put forward as a propitiation by his blood, to be received by faith" (Rom 3:23-25).

To settle the argument, and since he is talking to Jews, Paul goes back to Abraham, the founding father of the Jews, to show that justification is by faith alone. Essentially, he argues that whether you lived 2000 years before Christ (like Abraham did), or after Christ, like we do, you are justified before God in exactly the same way: by faith in the promises of God apart from works of the law.

> What then shall we say was gained by Abraham, our forefather according to the flesh? For if Abraham was justified by works, he has something to boast about, but not before God. For what does the Scripture say? "Abraham believed God, and it was counted to him as righteousness." Now to the one who works, his wages are not counted as a gift but as his due. And to the one who does not work but trusts him who justifies the ungodly, his faith is counted as righteousness ... (Rom 4:1-5)

Firstly, Paul says that justification comes to us as a *gift* and not a wage. The very nature of gifts is that they are not earned—they come to us freely, out of the generosity of the giver. We don't work for them. Instead, says Paul, the one who is justified (or 'counted as righteous') is the one who does not work, but simply trusts in "him who justifies the ungodly".

This is the astonishing news of the gospel: that God justifies not the good or the moral or the hard-working or the deserving but "the ungodly". Paul is very explicit about it. He says that justification comes to "one who does not work". We Australians have a word for those who choose not to work: we call them 'bludgers'. The apostle is saying in effect that justification is only for those who are prepared to 'bludge' on the mercy of God. In other words, it is for those who realize that their good works will never justify them before God, no matter how hard they try, and so who trust God and take him at his word rather than trust their good works.

To further demonstrate the point, Paul retraces Abraham's story and asks whether God declared Abraham to be justified before or after he was circumcised (circumcision being one of the classic 'works of the law'). Did the good work of circumcision play a part in his justification or not? The answer is No! God declared Abraham to be righteous simply because he trusted God's word.

When Luther and the other Reformers read Romans, they realized that the situation Paul was addressing was very similar to the one they faced with Roman Catholicism—a system in which God's grace and the work of Christ had some place, but where doing good works and keeping the laws (of the Church) were also absolutely necessary to merit salvation. They saw that the 'works' which will never justify were not simply the Old Testament works such as circumcision, but any human law or work (such as those imposed by the Church) that supposedly merited our justification.

Now at the time of the Reformation, the accusation that was thrown back at Luther and the others was exactly the same as Paul received in Romans: "What then? Are we to sin because we are not under law but under grace?" (Rom 6:15). In other words, if justification is by faith alone, apart from works of the law, doesn't that mean we can just sin as much as we like and then be forgiven? Won't justification by faith alone result in de-motivated Christians who aren't concerned for holiness?

Paul's answer (and Luther's) was absolutely and definitely not! The very purpose for which Christ has redeemed us, and freely justified us, is *so that* we might live a new life of godliness and holiness. We have been released from our slavery to sin, says Paul in Romans 6, *so that* we may serve a new master called "obedience". We don't do good works in order to earn our freedom; we do good works *because* we have been set free to do them. Paul makes the same point in his letter to the Ephesians:

> For by grace you have been saved through faith. And this is not your own doing; it is the gift of God, not a result of works, so that no one may boast. For we are his workmanship, created in Christ Jesus for good works, which God prepared beforehand, that we should walk in them. (Eph 2:8-10)

Our good works play no part in our being acceptable to God—that is, justified and saved. But they do play a big part in our lives, because the very reason God has resurrected us to new life in Christ is so that we might do all the holy and good things he has already prepared for us to do!

What is 'faith'?

If justification is by faith alone, what do we mean by the word 'faith'?

Simply put, faith is a personal attitude of trust and dependency. In fact, the word 'trust' is a good everyday replacement for 'faith' in most places where you meet the word in the Bible. Faith is by no means just an intellectual assent that something is true. It is a personal trust that something is true. But trust in what?

"Some trust in chariots and some in horses," says the psalmist, "but we trust in the name of the LORD our God" (Ps 20:7).

'Faith' in the Bible is trust *in God*, and especially in the promises of God—such as those promises that come to us in the gospel. Faith is an open hand ready to receive what God promises to give us through Christ. By its nature, faith offers nothing and contributes nothing. It simply trusts in Another, and receives salvation from him as a free gift. Faith points away from itself and says, "I can't take away my own sins, or atone for them. Christ alone can do that for me."

Abraham modelled that faith by taking God at his word. In Romans 4, Abraham's faith is defined in terms of being "*fully convinced that God was able to do what he had promised*" (Rom 4:21). Faith is about taking God at his word. And this, says Paul, is the only way a person can be justified—not through doing sufficient good works to earn God's approval, but by *putting our trust* in what Jesus has done on the cross to wipe out all our sins. Just as Abraham believed God's promise that he would have a son and be a father to many nations, and this rendered him 'righteous' in God's sight, so we also are 'counted righteous' by putting our trust in the death of Jesus:

> No distrust made [Abraham] waver concerning the promise
> of God, but he grew strong in his faith as he gave glory to
> God, fully convinced that God was able to do what he had
> promised. That is why his faith was "counted to him as
> righteousness". But the words "it was counted to him" were
> not written for his sake alone, but for ours also. It will be
> counted to us who believe in him who raised from the dead
> Jesus our Lord, who was delivered up for our trespasses
> and raised for our justification. (Rom 4:20-25)

Justified now ... saved then

God not only wants to save his people, he also wants them to
know they are saved. Paul notes that the reason why God
announces to Abraham that he is justified, well before he is
circumcised, is not just for his benefit but for ours as well.
God wants *us* to know with certainty that if we too trust the
promise that Christ died for our sins and was raised for our
justification, then we too are justified now.

Paul rams home the implications of this in the next chapter
(Romans 5). If we can know that we are justified *now*—that is,
if we can be sure that our guilt has been washed completely
away, and that we are quite blameless and righteous before
God because of Christ's sacrifice—then we can be sure that
we will have nothing to worry about on Judgement Day.
Here's how he puts it:

> For while we were still weak, at the right time Christ died
> for the ungodly. For one will scarcely die for a righteous
> person—though perhaps for a good person one would dare
> even to die—but God shows his love for us in that while we

were still sinners, Christ died for us. *Since, therefore, we have now been justified by his blood, much more shall we be saved by him from the wrath of God.* (Rom 5:6-9)

This is why a Bible-believing Christian can put his hand up in class and say, "Yes, I'm quite certain that if I died tonight, God would accept me into his eternal kingdom—not because I think I'm particularly good, or measure up to his standards, or have earned it, but because I'm placing my trust in Christ and his blood, and I know that God will definitely accept me on that basis, *because he has promised to*".

Tragically, Roman Catholicism rejects this view of justification. The Council of Trent declared: "If anyone says that the faith which justifies is nothing else but trust in the divine mercy, which pardons sin because of Christ; or that it is trust alone by which we are justified: let him be anathema". [3]

The tragedy of this rejection is not just that it flies in the face of what Paul teaches in Romans. The tragedy is that it robs Catholics of one of the greatest blessings of the gospel—the sweet peace and joy and assurance of knowing that our sins are completely dealt with in Christ, that we are freely justified before God through his blood, and that we can look forward with confidence to standing before God and being saved, not through our works, but through our trust in Christ alone.

In my own search for the truth about Christianity and Catholicism, this was one of the key issues. I realized that I was a sinner on a roller coaster to hell, and that there was only way of salvation—through Christ my saviour, who taken my place by dying on the cross.

I'm no Martin Luther, but I guess my experience was something like his. Here's how he described his conversion:

Though I lived as a monk without reproach, I felt that I was a sinner before God with an extremely disturbed conscience. I could not believe that he was placated by my satisfaction. I did not love, yes, I hated the righteous God who punishes sinners, and secretly, if not blasphemously, certainly murmuring greatly, I was angry with God ...

Thus I raged with a fierce and troubled conscience. Nevertheless, I beat importunately upon Paul at that place, most ardently desiring to know what St Paul wanted. At last, by the mercy of God, meditating day and night, I gave heed to the context of the words, namely, "In it the righteousness of God is revealed, as it is written, 'He who through faith is righteous shall live'". There I began to understand that the righteousness of God is that by which the righteous lives by a gift of God, namely by faith. And this is the meaning: the righteousness of God is revealed by the gospel, namely, the passive righteousness with which the merciful God justifies us by faith, as it is written, "He who through faith is righteous shall live". Here I felt that I was altogether born again and had entered paradise itself through open gates. There a totally other face of the entire Scripture showed itself to me ... And I extolled my sweetest word with a love as great as the hatred with which I had before hated the word "righteousness of God". Thus that place in Paul was for me truly the gate to paradise.[4]

When I grasped what God had freely done for me through Jesus, and that it was a gift from start to finish, and that all I could do was kneel with an open hand and receive the gift in faith—then, like Martin Luther, truly "I felt that I was altogether born again and had entered paradise itself through open gates".

Chapter 6
⊕ It's just grace

SEVERAL YEARS AGO, I preached at a midweek church service in the city of Sydney on being 'saved by grace' (Eph 2:8-9). On my way to the church, I passed the Grace Hotel. Not wanting to let a sermon illustration slip by, I went up to the concierge and asked if he had any rooms for free. He smiled and immediately said, "None!" Obviously the hotel was named after a person, not as a theological statement about God's free gift of salvation.

CS Lewis was right when he said that that the one belief unique to Christianity over and against every other world religion is *grace*. Salvation within Christianity is a work of God not man from beginning to end, and is given freely and undeservedly through Christ. Grace is generosity. It's when something is given purely out of the goodness and kindness of the giver, regardless of the worthiness of the recipient— indeed despite the *unworthiness* of the recipient.

'Grace' was a huge issue at the time of the Reformation. Over the last three chapters, we have looked at three very significant differences between Reformation-style Protestantism and Catholicism. Ever since the time of the Reformation, Protestants have summarized these three core areas of difference in three slogans or catchcries:

⊕ *Christ alone* (not Christ plus human priests and the sacrifice of the Mass)

⊕ *Bible alone* (not the Bible plus the traditions and authority of the church)

⊕ *faith alone* (not faith plus our good works and merits as the basis of salvation).

To these three slogans, the Reformers added one more: *grace alone*. And in a sense, *grace alone* summarizes and explains the other three:

⊕ Christ alone is the way to the Father, and Christ comes from outside, purely and only because of the kindness and love of God. We don't earn him. We don't contribute to his work, or help him finish it off (through human priests and the Mass). Christ does it all, entirely through the generosity of God—through grace.

⊕ Likewise with the Bible. The word of God comes to us from outside, and stands as God's gracious gift to us, to teach and encourage and correct and rebuke and train us. We should humbly and gladly accept the gracious word that comes to us from God, and submit to it—not attempt to add our own traditions and teachings to it.

⊕ It's the same with salvation and faith. Justification is a gift from God, given freely in Christ. Our response is nothing more than an open hand, held out in trust, that grasps hold of the wonderful promises of the gospel. We don't *deserve* to be justified or saved. We are not saved by our merits or works or contribution in any way, but by grace.

Even our capacity for responding to God—even the ability to turn to him and to accept his forgiveness—even that is a gift of God, because of ourselves and by ourselves, we are incapable. Here is Paul again, in a very important passage:

> And you were dead in the trespasses and sins in which you once walked, following the course of this world, following the prince of the power of the air, the spirit that is now at work in the sons of disobedience—among whom we all once lived in the passions of our flesh, carrying out the desires of the body and the mind, and were by nature children of wrath, like the rest of mankind. But God, being rich in mercy, because of the great love with which he loved us, even when we were dead in our trespasses, made us alive together with Christ—by grace you have been saved— and raised us up with him and seated us with him in the heavenly places in Christ Jesus, so that in the coming ages he might show the immeasurable riches of his grace in kindness toward us in Christ Jesus. For by grace you have been saved through faith. And this is not your own doing; it is the gift of God, not a result of works, so that no one may boast. For we are his workmanship, created in Christ Jesus for good works, which God prepared beforehand, that we should walk in them. (Eph 2:1-10)

Notice what Paul says here. It's not that we were spiritually sick or weak. We didn't need healing or assistance. Our condition was far worse than that. As far as God was concerned, we were stone cold dead—"dead in the trespasses and sins" that were the normal practice of our daily lives. We followed not God but "the prince of the power of the air" (that is, Satan), who was at work in us. We were slaves to the passions and desires of our body and mind, and were "by nature children of wrath". It's the bleakest of bleak pictures.

But—and you've got to love the word 'but' in that sentence!—*but* God, being rich in mercy and love, breathed new life into our dead spiritual carcases. He raised us up to new life, "even when we were dead in our trespasses". And in case we'd missed the point, Paul emphasizes it twice: "by *grace* you have been saved".

I love the way Bob Dylan basically summarizes Paul in his song, *Saved*:

> I was blinded by the devil,
> Born already ruined,
> Stone-cold dead
> As I stepped out of the womb.
>
> By His grace I have been touched,
> By His word I have been healed,
> By His hand I've been delivered,
> By His spirit I've been sealed.
> I've been saved
> By the blood of the lamb ...

The Protestant Reformers perceived that this teaching from the Bible about 'grace' constituted a major difference from Roman Catholicism.

Roman Catholicism does believe in 'grace', and teaches

'grace', but its understanding of the word is complex, and is often different from what the Bible means by it. According to Catholicism, 'grace' is not only God's free favour and generosity; it is also a kind of power or assistance which God gives to help us. The initial grace of forgiveness and cleansing that God grants us, and which for the Catholic occurs at baptism, cannot be earned or merited. But the 'graces' God supplies throughout the rest of the Christian life *can be* merited, according to Catholicism: "[W]e can then merit for ourselves and for others the graces needed for our sanctification, for the increase of grace and charity, and for the attainment of eternal life".[1]

It may seem strange or contradictory that 'grace' can be merited, but it is quite consistent with Catholicism's tendency to see salvation in all its different aspects as an act of cooperation between man and God. God, for his part, is kind and merciful; man, for his part, tries hard to merit God's kindness through good works. 'Grace' is the outcome, a partly merited gift. It comes from God's kindness, and imparts God's power to us, but the cooperation of the human, and the Church in particular, is still essential.

At a deeper level, this view of the cooperation of man in grace is built on Catholicism's view of man, which is more optimistic than the Protestant view. According to Catholic teaching, man is fallen and sinful, but it doesn't go all the way down. Something was lost at the fall, but much of man's essential nature remains intact, and is capable of reaching out to and responding to God. In opposition to the Reformed view, the Council of Trent stated that adults "who by sins were alienated from God, may be disposed through His quickening and assisting grace, to convert themselves to their own justification, by freely assenting to and cooperating with that said grace".[2]

So for Protestantism, man is spiritually dead, and salvation is all through God's unmerited favour (his 'grace'); for Catholicism, man is spiritually weak and fallen, but with some assistance from God (some special power or 'grace') is capable of cooperating with God's call, and meriting further 'grace' through good works.

This goes back to what we discovered about justification and salvation in our previous chapter. In Protestantism, justification happens once—it's a once-for-all declaration by God of 'not guilty' on the sinner, because of the once-for-all sacrifice of Christ. In Catholicism, justification is a process which happens over time, involving the imparting of righteousness by God in cooperation with the believer.

The sacraments and grace

Roman Catholicism is a sacramental religion. The whole of a Catholic's life, from the womb to the tomb, and beyond into purgatory, is shaped by the seven sacraments: Baptism, Confirmation, Eucharist, Penance, Anointing of the Sick, Holy Orders and Matrimony.[3]

The sacraments are the chief means by which the 'graces' of God are imparted to the believer so that the process of justification can continue: "Our sacraments both contain grace and confer it on those who receive them worthily".[4] By duly and worthily participating in the sacraments, the believer receives grace, and so grows in sanctification and righteousness, in the hope that he or she will be justified finally at the last.

Thus, the sacraments are non-negotiable for Catholics: they are necessary for salvation, and mediate the grace of salvation at every stage of the believer's life.[5] The sacrament of Baptism (usually for infants) removes the stain of original sin, and regenerates the child as a truly righteous, justified member of God's family. Confirmation (usually occurring at around age 10) confers the outpouring of the Holy Spirit, uniting the Catholic more fully to Christ. Exactly what is added in Confirmation that is not gained in Baptism is a source of some discussion within Catholicism, but the 'process' element of justification is clearly evident. Throughout the believer's life, the sacrament of Penance (sometimes also called Confession or Reconciliation) enables mortal sins to be forgiven.[6] In the sacrament of the Eucharist, which ought to be taken at least weekly, the priest offers on the congregation's behalf the sacrifice by which sins are atoned for, and by partaking of the sacrament the believer receives the grace of Christ. If one marries or is ordained to the priesthood, the grace required for these states of life is again channelled through the sacraments of Matrimony or Holy Orders. And as death approaches, the priest will come and offer the Anointing of the Sick (the 'last rites' or 'extreme unction' as it also called).

Thus, although Catholicism uses the language of 'grace' and 'justification', a very different picture emerges. And the Reformers saw this:

> [W]here Rome had taught a piecemeal salvation, to be
> gained by stages through working a sacramental treadmill,

the Reformers now proclaimed a unitary salvation, to be received in its entirety here and now by self-abandoning faith in God's promise, and in the God and the Christ of that promise, as set forth in the pages of the Bible.[7]

Through hearing the gospel and being united to Christ through faith, believers receive all of his blessings—complete and free forgiveness of all our sins, the gift and seal of the Holy Spirit who leads and enables us to live a godly life, adoption as God's children, citizenship in heaven, the sure hope of eternal life, and so on. It comes as a complete package, entirely as a gift to be received by faith, as a result of God's grace or generosity alone, and not our merits or works.

In Catholicism, by contrast, salvation is piecemeal, incomplete and uncertain, and requires the constant work of the believer. Grace comes in stages through human activity— that is, through the sacraments—over the course of a lifetime, with the uncertain hope that sufficient righteousness will have been imparted and earned to merit salvation at the end.

In practice, this means that the life of the devoted Catholic is one of ritual obligation and performance. The message I received growing up, and which Catholics all over the world receive, was: Keep going to mass, keep going to confession, be a good Catholic, and you'll give yourself the best chance of going to heaven. The focus was all on what *I had to do*, and this seems to be the inevitable result of the Catholic sacramental system.

Going to confession was a case in point. There were three things you had to do in order to have sins forgiven through confession: confess to the priest what you'd done, be genuinely sorry for what you'd done, and then, after the priest had absolved you, make 'satisfaction' for your sins. This satisfaction or 'penance' could take the form of saying certain prayers, doing works of mercy, helping a neighbour, undertaking some form of self-denial, and so on. It was very common in my youth for the priest to set a penance of saying three 'Hail Marys'.[8]

It was not only on my own behalf that I was required to do certain things to make up for sins. I also remember going to special masses on behalf of departed relatives, to shorten their time in purgatory. According to Catholic teaching, because justification is a process of making someone more righteous until they are finally deemed fit for heaven, that process may not be finished when the person dies. And so the process of purification continues after death, in an intermediate state called 'purgatory'.[9] Purgatory is different from hell; purgatory is only for believers who are on their way to heaven, but who are required to undergo purification (in an unspecified manner) for a certain period of time. Time in purgatory can be shortened by prayers, alms, masses and works of penance undertaken by those still on earth, or indeed by obtaining an indulgence.

The clear assumption of the doctrine of purgatory is that Jesus' death is not enough to cleanse the believer from the consequences of sin. This is the price that is paid for abandoning the biblical concept of justification by faith alone. We only need to recall the promise of immediate salvation to the thief on the cross, who had committed the mortal sin of murder. He heard these marvellous words from Jesus' mouth: "Truly, I say to you, today you will be with me in Paradise" (Luke 23:43). Presumably the penitent thief did not have to endure purgatory and experience temporal consequences for his mortal or venial sins. It appears that trusting the promise of Jesus was enough.

As I LOOKED BACK ON ALL THIS, and examined the Catholic Church's teaching, it became very clear to me that the Catholic language of 'grace' disguised an elaborate man-made religious system that was much more about merit, works and performance than free grace. Where in the Bible is there even the faintest hint of an idea like purgatory? Let alone the concept that people on earth can help others get into heaven more quickly by doing good works on their behalf?!

Purgatory is yet another late addition to the Church's teaching, decreed to be part of the tradition of the Church by the Councils of Florence (1439) and Trent (1547-63). One can only feel for those believers who had died in the previous 1400 years, thinking that Christ's death had paid for their sins, only to get a nasty surprise—"Sorry, it seems like you'll have to work off the punishment for some of your sins yourself".

If it all sounds a million miles from the teaching of the New Testament about Christ and salvation, it's because it is! When Paul declares that it is "by grace you have been saved through faith. And this is not your own doing; it is the gift of God, not a result of works, so that no one may boast" (Eph 2:8-9)—is it even remotely conceivable that he had in mind something like the elaborate system of Catholicism, where 'grace' is dispensed by priests through the performance of certain rituals?

If I sound passionate about this, it's because I am! I came to this realization not out of idle religious curiosity, or because I like an argument, or because I was particularly bitter about my Catholic upbringing. I came to it with tears, and with agony, because I knew that to reject Catholicism was to reject my family and my culture.

But I realized in the end that I had no choice. The truth matters because God matters. And the truth, in the end, is a matter of salvation. As I delved into the teaching of Catholicism, I saw that at every point in the system, the finality and sufficiency of Christ's death for my sins was played down or compromised; free forgiveness was given with one hand, but taken away again with the other, depending on my performance; and the assurance of my place in God's kingdom, through the death of Christ alone, was denied to me.

I saw that rather than God's salvation being a gift of his grace alone, to be gratefully received through faith alone, salvation in Catholicism was an act of collaboration, which relied in part on human works to attract God's favour and to make satisfaction for one's failures.

When my father went back to Malta ten years ago, he met his former school teacher, who was well into his nineties. After my father explained that his son had become an Anglican minister, the teacher said: "Do you know, Tom, why they don't believe in purgatory? It's because they believe God is so kind that he will take his people straight into heaven."

When my father told me about this, I thought to myself, "What an insightful comment!"

The sheer kindness or grace of God expressed in the sufficient work of Christ at the cross means that death becomes the doorway not into purgatory, but into the loving presence of God.

Chapter 7
⊕ Mary

I WAS VISITING MY MOTHER recently when there was a knock at the door. A couple were standing there, but they were not Jehovah's Witnesses, nor even some keen door-knocking evangelicals. They were from the Legion of Mary, an organization set up to promote devotion to the mother of Jesus.

Perhaps one of the most surprising things for me when I started to mix with non-Catholic Christians was to discover how little they cared about Mary.

It can be hard for non-Catholics to appreciate just how precious Mary is to many traditional Roman Catholics. In fact, while having a 'personal relationship with Jesus' is considered a bit odd by many Catholics, having a personal relationship with Mary is not. Mary is the Mother—the Mother of Christ, the Mother of God, the Mother of all Christians everywhere—and her place in Catholic devotion remains undiminished.

Pope John Paul II credited Mary with saving him from an assassin's bullet in 1981 because it happened on the first anniversary of an apparition of Mary at Fatima.

In our investigation of the differences between Protestantism and Catholicism, it's worth taking a chapter to think about Mary—not just because Marian devotion is such an obvious difference between the two, but because in many ways the controversy about Mary sums up many of the themes we have been looking at.

Let's start by sketching out what the Bible itself says about Mary.

Mary in the New Testament

We first meet Mary in the Gospels as a young girl, a virgin, engaged to Joseph. She responds with faith and praise to the angelic news that she will bear a special child—unlike Zechariah, who did not take the angel's word at face value. She is clearly an extraordinary young woman, and the privilege she receives of giving birth to the Saviour means that "all generations will call [her] blessed" (Luke 1:48).

She gives birth to Jesus while still a virgin—the Bible is quite clear on this—although she has normal marital relations with Joseph subsequently. Matthew's Gospel tells us that Joseph "knew her not *until* she had given birth to a son" (Matt 1:25), and Jesus' siblings are referred to at numerous points in the Gospels (e.g. Matt 13:55; Mark 3:31, 6:3; John 7:3-5). Along with Joseph, Mary raises Jesus, presenting him at the temple as the law required (Luke 2:22-23), pondering his destiny in her heart (Luke 2:19, 51), and experiencing normal maternal concern when Jesus goes missing on the trip back to Nazareth (Luke 2:41-50).

We hear almost nothing of Mary during Jesus' ministry. We see her making a request of him at the wedding of Cana, to which Jesus responds rather curtly ("Woman, what does this have to do with me?")—although he then does what Mary asks (John 2:1-11). At another point, Mary comes with Jesus' brothers to persuade him to come home with them, out of concern for his wellbeing. Jesus dismisses their concern (Mark 3:20-35).

We next see Mary with the other women at the crucifixion of Jesus. From the cross, Jesus entrusts Mary to the care of 'the beloved disciple' (that is, John; John 19:25-27). She is found praying with the other apostles in the upper room prior to Pentecost as one of the 120 disciples (Acts 1:14).

Mary in the unwritten traditions of the Church

The extraordinary body of belief and devotional practice that has grown up around Mary over the past 2000 years has very little in the Bible to rest on. The Catholic Church admits this. It doesn't pretend that its distinctive teaching on Mary is explicitly found in the Bible. Rather, the Church "has recognized and defined certain beliefs about Mary that are found implicitly in the Bible (not in their full form)".[1]

These are the oral traditions we looked at in chapter 4, that have grown and developed over time, and have been given the Catholic Church's stamp of approval as a true part of God's revelation to us.

Let's look at some of these traditions.

Mary the mother of God

At the Council of Ephesus in 431 AD, aspects of the nature of Christ were debated. As a kind of test case in this debate, it was decided that Mary should be given the title *theotokos* (meaning 'mother of God' or 'God-bearer')—because if Jesus was fully God as well as fully man, then it could be said that his human mother was 'giving birth to God'. The debate was about the nature and status of Jesus, not the status of Mary, but this decision was subsequently used to justify veneration of and devotion to Mary.

The perpetual virginity of Mary

Roman Catholicism teaches not only that Mary gave birth to Jesus as a virgin, but that she remained a virgin for the rest of her life, with Jesus as her only son. Faced with the multiple references to Jesus' brothers and sisters in the Gospels, Catholicism says that these could have been step-brothers, or possibly cousins—although even some Catholic authors admit that these are exceedingly weak arguments.[2]

Insisting on Mary's perpetual virginity is strange for another reason: it implies that sexuality within marriage is somehow unspiritual or defiling, as if it would have sullied Mary in some way. But sex within marriage is God's good and holy gift, and the biblical pattern for marriage—"and they shall become one flesh" (Gen 2:24). In fact, the Bible goes so far as to say that it is wrong for husbands or wives to deny each other sexually (1 Cor 7:4-5).

Catholicism says that Mary's perpetual virginity is a "sign of her total consecration to God and of respect for the fact that God himself had dwelt and grown within her womb".[3]

But in what sense is virginity a sign of consecration or devotion to God? Does this mean that Moses, who had a wife and children, was not totally devoted to the Lord? Or that the Apostle Peter, who also was married, was not worthy of a part in God's plan?[4]

Mary the mother of the Church

The teaching of Mary's perpetual virginity flows into the idea of Mary as the mother of the Church: "Mary was also being called by God to be the mother of all Christians, who have been made Christ's body through baptism".[5]

Interestingly, there is no hint in the New Testament that Mary should be thought of in this way. After the mention of her presence with the 120 disciples in Acts 1, Mary disappears from the pages of the New Testament. In the rest of the book of Acts, she plays no role whatsoever in the story of the growing church. In the remaining 22 books of the New Testament, which teach so much about God's plans, the nature of the church, and the Christian life, Mary is completely absent.

Indeed, if anything, the New Testament warns about giving Mary too prominent a place. Note the words of Jesus in Luke's Gospel:

> As he said these things, a woman in the crowd raised her voice and said to him, "Blessed is the womb that bore you, and the breasts at which you nursed!" But he said, "Blessed rather are those who hear the word of God and keep it!"
> (Luke 11:27-28)

Here, surely, was the perfect opportunity for Jesus to affirm the high value and place of his mother in God's plan of salvation, and to direct his disciples to honour and venerate her. Instead, he gently rebukes the woman who wants to praise Mary. The ultimate blessing, says Jesus, is not carrying Jesus in the womb, but carrying God's word in your heart.

There is absolutely no biblical warrant for regarding Mary as the mother of all Christians. And yet for Catholics, this teaching is very important. For many Catholics, Mary is like a heavenly, spiritual mum, and they are very sensitive to pleasing or grieving her. They cast their cares before her, and look to her to intercede for them with her Son. The tenderness of Mary's mediation is captured in a prayer I memorized as an eight-year-old:

> Hail, Holy Queen, Mother of Mercy, our life, our sweetness, and our hope. To you do we cry, poor banished children of Eve. To you do we send up our sighs, mourning and weeping in this valley of tears. Turn then, O most gracious advocate, your eyes of mercy toward us and after this our exile show unto us the blessed fruit of your womb, Jesus. O clement! O loving! O sweet Virgin Mary! Pray for us, O Holy Mother of God, that we may be made worthy of the promises of Christ.

Contrast this prayer with the words of the book of Hebrews, as it talks about how Jesus was made just like us, sharing our flesh and blood, and experiencing suffering and temptation:

> For we do not have a high priest who is unable to sympathize with our weaknesses, but one who in every respect has been tempted as we are, yet without sin. Let us then with confidence draw near to the throne of grace, that we may receive mercy and find grace to help in time of need. (Heb 4:15-16)

In Jesus we have a mediator and a friend, to whom we can go for help and grace in our time of need. In Catholicism, Mary has largely replaced Jesus in this role. She is to be our first port of call—we go to her for help and grace and mercy, in the hope that she will put a good word in for us with her Son. Christ's role as intercessor, mediator and friend of sinners becomes blurred and sidelined.

The immaculate conception of Mary

But Catholic teaching about Mary does not end there. The Catholic doctrine of the immaculate conception states that "in view of Mary's role of bearing and raising the Son of God, God prepared her for this by freeing her from original sin from the moment of her conception in the womb of her mother, Anne. God prepared Mary to be a vessel without a trace of sin, not because of her own virtue or merit but because of her unique role in her plan of salvation."[6] In other words, Mary did not share in original sin with the rest of humanity and remained sinless throughout her life.

Again, not only does this tradition have no support in the Scriptures, it clashes with what we do know from the Scriptures. Christ is repeatedly affirmed as being without sin in the New Testament; Mary never is. In fact, the testimony of Jesus is that "no one is good except God alone" (Mark 10:18); and Paul says that "all have sinned and fall short of the glory of God" (Rom 3:23). The picture that the New Testament builds up of Mary is that she was a faithful, godly woman, but that like all the godly heroes of the Bible she was still a member of our sinful human race.

Catholicism places Mary on a sinless, virginal and

maternal pedestal apart from other believers because it wishes to carve out a place for Mary as the Holy Mother, the Queen of Heaven, the special mediator who stands between us and her Son, and represents us to him.

The assumption of Mary

Popular Catholic devotion to Mary has grown over the centuries. In the middle of the last century, millions of petitions were submitted, begging the Pope to define as infallible dogma the 'Assumption of Mary' into heaven. This finally happened in 1950, when Pope Pius XII declared that Mary, "having completed the course of her earthly life, was assumed body and soul into heavenly glory".[7] She receives her resurrection body at the end of her life and, given her sinless life, avoids purgatory and enters heaven. It remains unclear whether the Catholic Church teaches that Mary first experienced bodily death.

Significantly, says one Catholic writer, "The Assumption of Mary is a source of hope for us because it foreshadows what will one day happen to each faithful Christian".[8] Mary's receiving of her resurrected body before Judgement Day is a foreshadowing of every Christian's hope.

However, according to the New Testament, this is precisely the function that Christ's resurrection is meant to perform:

> For as in Adam all die, so also in Christ shall all be made
> alive. But each in his own order: Christ the firstfruits, then
> at his coming those who belong to Christ. (1 Cor 15:22-23)

Christ is the one who blazes the trail for Christians, who as the 'Last Adam' defeats death and rises to new life as the first of a new resurrected race. His resurrection as a man is the guarantee of our resurrection. And that resurrection happens on the last day, not before (cf. Phil 3:10-21).

Once again, we find the unique place and role of Christ being impinged upon by the Catholic view of Mary. Our minds are drawn away from Jesus and his resurrection to Mary. And nowhere is this more clear than in Mary's role as mediatrix.

Mary as mediatrix and co-redemptrix[9]

As the mother of all Christians, Mary is said to pray and intercede for each of her children and for the Church as a whole. Speaking of her role as mediator, Pope John Paul II writes,

> Mary places herself between her Son and mankind in
> the reality of their wants, needs and suffering. She puts
> herself 'in the middle'—that is to say, she acts as a
> mediatrix not as an outsider, but in her position as mother.
> She knows that as such she can point out to her Son the
> needs of mankind, and in fact, she 'has the right' to do so.
> Her meditation is thus in the nature of intercession ...[10]

Roman Catholicism affirms on the one hand the uniqueness of Christ as mediator, and yet paradoxically undermines the same truth by its portrayal of Mary as mediator. In fact, Mary is even given the title 'co-redemptrix' because she cooperated with Christ in the redemption of the world by her consent to bear Jesus. Mary's obedience is viewed as a necessary step in God's plan to save his people. Then, at the cross, Mary's intense sufferings, united with those of her Son, provide "a contribution to the Redemption of us all".[11]

Within Catholicism, there seems to be no place where

Christ is left alone to do his work of salvation. Or to put it another way, there is no place where Mary as the representative of humanity does not lay claim to Christ's uniqueness. Mary shares Christ's sinless purity, his obedience to the Father's will, his redemptive work, his resurrected body, and his mediation and heavenly intercession.

Growing up, like so many Catholics I was told that we present our requests to God through Mary in the same way as we ask our earthly mothers to present our requests to our fathers, who can be rather stern and distant. I am now astonished that I did not see the implications of speaking in these terms—because it surely both dishonours God the Father, who loved us so much that he gave his one and only Son for us, and undermines Christ, who enables us to draw near to the throne of grace with boldness. There is no escaping this: to insert someone else in the role of mediator says either that God the Father is still angry, or that God the Son is inadequate.

Practice always shapes theology. In the Rosary, for example, the sheer number of prayers directed to Mary as opposed to the Father fosters the dominance of Mary.[12] For every Lord's Prayer there are ten Hail Marys. And while Catholics are encouraged to meditate on Christ's ministry, the Rosary ends with a meditation on the assumption of Mary and the coronation of Mary as queen of heaven.

We have not space here to discuss the myriad forms of devotion to Mary that have evolved over the centuries—wearing special medals or necklaces that will ensure Mary's protection, the pilgrimages to sites where apparitions of Mary are said to have appeared, and so on.

Mary as the essence of Catholicism

The Catholic teaching about Mary sums up in many respects the key problems with Catholicism. The influential German theologian Karl Barth put it this way: "In the doctrine and worship of Mary there is disclosed the one heresy of the Roman Catholic Church which explains all the rest. The 'mother of God' of Roman Catholic Marian dogma is quite simply the principle, type and essence of *the human creature participating servant-like in its own redemption*" (emphasis added).[13]

The human creature participating servant-like in its own redemption—those are penetrating words. Not by Christ alone as found in the Bible alone, and received by faith alone, through grace alone. For Catholicism, the human must always be re-inserted, whether it is the role of human priests in the Mass, or the role of the Church in determining the word of God, or the role of our works in meriting salvation.

And the Catholic teaching about Mary is a classic example. We see Christ's uniqueness shunted to one side and his human mother stepping up alongside him to take on the role of mediator and friend of sinners; we see the Bible being swamped by the gradual addition of infallible Church traditions that are ever more removed from what the Bible actually teaches; and we see prayers and devotions to Mary being practised in order to gain her favour and protection.

The heart of the problem is the desire by humans to participate in their own salvation, and the institutionalization of this desire in the teaching and practice of the Catholic Church.

Chapter 8
⊕ It is finished

YOU HAVE TO FEEL for my wife, Sandy.

I'm Maltese. Sandy isn't. And people say that we Maltese have only two volume levels: off and loud. When I have an opinion, I tend to shout it. I think my wife must be a very patient woman.

I mention this because I hope that as you've been reading this book, you haven't been put off by my tendency to shout an opinion. I've done my best to remain cool and dispassionate in discussing Catholicism and the critique of Catholicism by Bible-based Protestants. But it's not easy to do so. When the truth you are seeking is a person, and when the consequences of your quest are so massive, remaining completely cool and calm isn't always possible. It matters too much.

The truth is, I find it hard to remain cool about Catholicism, because as a newly converted Christ-follower looking hard at my Catholic heritage, I kept running up against painful but unavoidable contradictions. At almost every point where Catholicism taught something distinctive, the effect of the teaching was to undermine the person and work of the Christ I had come to love, and wanted to honour and serve.

This upset and disturbed me. It still does.

We've looked at numerous examples in the course of this book. We saw, for example, how the Catholic Mass takes the focus off Christ, the great high priest who made the one final and sufficient sacrifice, and puts it instead on human priests re-offering Christ on the altar (in the bread and wine) as an atoning sacrifice. We looked at how the Church of Rome places itself between the believer and God, as the mediator of revelation—as the authoritative interpreter of Scripture, and as the determiner of which Church traditions and teachings will be given the status of the 'word of God'. It is not Christ speaking directly to us through his Scriptural word, but the Church, led by the Pope, telling us what is and isn't God's word. We also considered how God's grace in Catholicism is not his free generosity to the sinner, granting forgiveness and justification only through the death of Christ and received by faith alone—but that grace is a kind of power or aid, which is channelled to believers through the sacraments of the church, so that they might be inwardly renewed and gradually become more righteous, and so be finally acceptable (or justified) at the last.

The underlying theme, expressed at every point, is the human desire to participate and collaborate: in Christ's work, in revelation, in salvation. As Barth so incisively put it: "the human creature participating servant-like in its own redemption". It's not that grace is missing, or faith is absent, or the Bible is ignored, or Christ is not crucial, but Catholicism seems to have an unrelenting need to find a place for the human; to insert the Church and its rituals and works into God's plan of salvation. "Let me just help", Catholicism seems to say. But the result, over centuries, has been a slow but inevitable usurping of the supremacy of God. Human mediation takes over. And so Christ's death becomes insufficient (we need the priests to repeat it in the Mass, and we need to work off some of the punishment ourselves in purgatory); the Bible becomes insufficient (we need the Church to interpret it, and to supplement it with its own teachings); the promise of the gospel becomes insufficient (we need to receive the Church's sacraments, and contribute our own works and merits).

Now some will rightly say that Catholicism has sought to reform itself through Vatican II, to curb some excesses, and to increase the role of Bible reading in the Mass and in the daily life of the Catholic. This is surely to be welcomed. I also rejoice that the increasing sense of openness and dialogue towards other denominations and religions post-Vatican II has seen many of the old sectarian battles of the past disappear. (And, of course, Protestants have played their role in the ugly conflicts of the past as well.)

However, it is hard to see the reforms of Vatican II as being driven by a return to the Bible. Vatican II encouraged the Church to believe *more* than what the Bible says on such topics as Mary, but also *less* than what the Bible says about other religions (see the Appendix for more on this). Under the pressure of theological liberalism, a degree of universalism has been seeping into the Church of Rome, and with it, somewhat ironically, a heightened sense of subjectivity when it comes to authority. These days, it is hard to know who speaks for the Catholic Church, even though officially it remains the Pope. There are many voices clamouring for attention.

The clearest evidence that Vatican II did not signal a return to Scripture for the Catholic Church is the continued exaltation of Mary in God's plan of salvation. Rather than letting go of biblically unfounded conclusions such as Mary's role as mother of the Church, her sinlessness, her perpetual virginity, and so on, the Catholic Church affirmed these doctrines, and has even added to them by highlighting Mary as co-redemptrix with Jesus.

It is really hard to know what is worse: to believe more than the Bible and so put words in the mouth of God, or to believe less than the Bible and ignore what God has said.

This undermining of the supremacy and sufficiency of Christ is not just theoretical. It percolates down to the daily lives of Catholics everywhere. I remember being asked by one lady whether it was all right to pray to St Jude. In a rare moment of thinking before speaking, I asked a question rather than blurted out an answer.

"Carmen," I said, "help me understand why you would want to do that?"

She said, "A couple of reasons, Ray. First, there are so many people in this world that surely God would be helped by having the saints receive some of the prayers for him."

I answered her by saying, "Carmen, does this sound like the God who upholds the universe by the power of his word and knows your needs even before you ask?"

She conceded, "I guess not".

"Is there another reason why you would want to pray to St Jude?"

"Well, I was hoping that St Jude could put in a good word for me if God is angry with me."

I said, "Does this sound like the God who loved you so much that he did not withhold his one and only Son?"

Again she conceded, "Not really!"

The idea of praying to the saints to help us, like praying to Mary, is just another example of a practice which not only has no biblical support, but is a slap in the face for Christ himself —as if *his* intercession is faulty or imperfect or inadequate; as if something else is needed, some human component, some other form of mediation, to get us there.

The ironic thing is that the New Testament itself warns us about this very problem. In the book of Hebrews, for example, the writer urges his readers in the strongest language not to go back to old covenant religion—with its provision of altars, priests, renewable sacrifices and tabernacles. The message is: don't regress into the shadows; the reality has come! New covenant Christianity is marked by the perfect sacrifice offered once for all by the perfect heavenly high priest before a perfect God in heaven making us perfect and blameless by faith. And so Hebrews calls on us to draw near to God with boldness and full assurance of faith because of the new and living way that has been opened for us through Christ's final and perfect sacrifice.

The parallels with Catholicism are obvious, not only in altars, priests, renewable sacrifices and tabernacles, but in the lack of boldness and assurance. The more that salvation depends on human contribution and participation, the more uncertain it is, and the more assurance evaporates. The joy of having God working *in* us by his Spirit transforming us from one degree of glory to the next can only be fully appreciated if we know that God is already *for* us, that he has already completely forgiven and justified us by the blood of his Son. We fear the Lord so that we can serve the Lord without fear. We know that we will be with him at the finish, because Christ has already cried out, "It is finished" (John 19:30).

It is for these reasons that I left the Catholic Church, and that I now call myself a 'Protestant'. I didn't do this to swap from one 'party' to another, like a Labor voter who has swung across to the Liberals. It's just that, for me, as I looked hard at what Catholicism teaches, I concluded that the Protestant Reformers were basically right. The arguments that I have put forward in earlier chapters about Christ, the Mass, the Bible and the Church, and the biblical truths of faith alone and grace alone, are essentially the arguments of the Reformation. And they remain the main obstacles to remaining within Roman Catholicism if you want to be a Christian who takes God at his word. The reasons Luther and all the others felt they had to break from Catholicism are essentially the reasons that I felt I also had to leave. Despite the many ways in which 21st-century Catholicism is different from the 15th-century version, in its essential doctrines and structure it remains unchanged (indeed, its 'unchangeableness' is part of its nature).

Now if you are reading this book as a Protestant, I hope it will have been helpful to you in a number of ways. I hope first of all that it has filled your heart all over again with the joy of knowing God through the gospel. I hope it has clarified what the differences are between Roman Catholicism and Protestant, Bible-based Christianity, and why being a 'Protestant' is just as important today as it was at the time of the Reformation. I hope it has helped you to understand your Catholic friends a little better.

One thing I'm hoping that this book *hasn't* done is inspire you to corner unsuspecting Catholics and beat them around the head with your new-found insights into Catholic theology. It does us good to remember that, like Paul, we preach Christ crucified and not some anti-Catholic message. This won't mean that these issues shouldn't be explored— there will be a right time and place for doing just that. But if we are going to argue for 'grace alone', we should speak with grace alone as well—that is, with gentleness, respect and love.

As a (now) Protestant relating to Catholics, I have found that there are practical implications that follow on from understanding Catholic doctrine and practice. For example, if I am invited to a Catholic wedding or a Catholic relative dies and mass is said, I always attend, but only participate in the first section of the 'liturgy of the Word'. As I noted in the first chapter, most of the prayers in this part of the Mass come from either the Bible or the early centuries of Christianity. But as the 'liturgy of the Eucharist' begins in the Mass, I respectfully sit down (which is not always easy) because I cannot with a clear conscience participate.

If you are a Catholic reading this book, I hope you have found it illuminating and challenging, not only about what your church teaches but about what the Bible teaches. It will come as no surprise for me to say that I hope you search the Scriptures for yourself to test what has been said against that authority. Don't take my word for it. Take up God's word and see for yourself.

Depending on the conclusions you come to, you may face a difficult decision—a decision that may feel like a betrayal of your family and culture. But our loyalty, in the end, must not be to our church or our parents but to the Lord Jesus Christ alone, who calls us to come to him alone for the forgiveness of our sins and to submit to his Lordship.

If you are persuaded that the distinctive teaching of the Catholic Church really does undermine Christ, and if you want to follow Christ, then you have little choice—even though you may be afraid of what others will think, say or do. God wants you to honour and serve his Son, whatever the cost.

For me, part of that cost was leaving the church of my family and my people. It was a cost measured in pain and tears. But it's a cost I would pay a thousand times over, because of the surpassing worth of knowing Christ Jesus my Lord, as the Apostle Paul said: "For his sake I have suffered the loss of all things and count them as rubbish, in order that I may gain Christ and be found in him, not having a righteousness of my own that comes from the law, but that which comes through faith in Christ, the righteousness from God that depends on faith" (Phil 3:8-10).

Appendix
⊕ The new Catholicism

Because of the field of Christian ministry that I work in, I often find myself talking to Roman Catholics about the differences between our faiths. Interestingly, the strongest reactions and noisiest arguments arise not as we talk about Mary, or discuss the infallibility of the Church, or debate the existence of purgatory, but when we touch on the exclusive claims of Christ and other religions. Nearly all Roman Catholics that I talk to are offended by the idea that salvation might only be found within Catholicism. They want to insist that sincere believers from other Christian denominations, and also from other religions like Islam, can also find salvation.

Now this is one area in which Catholicism has most definitely changed in recent times. The historic teaching of the Catholic Church was expressed in the Latin phrase *extra ecclesiam nulla salus*, meaning: "Outside the Church there is no salvation".[1] However, even before Vatican II it was clear that the Church was moving on this issue. In 1953, it excommunicated a Boston priest, Leonard Feeney, for insisting that people could only be saved by virtue of being baptized within the Catholic Church. At Vatican II, the Church formally recognized the validity of other Christian churches for the first time, affirming that:

⊕ all who are justified by faith through baptism are brothers in the Lord

⊕ all endowments that build up the church can exist outside the visible boundaries of the Catholic Church

⊕ brethren divided from the Catholic Church also carry out many of the sacred actions of the Christian religion

⊕ the Holy Spirit is at work in these church communities.[2]

While the Catholic Church acknowledged the defects in non-Catholic churches, they made it clear that such churches "have been by no means deprived of significance and importance in the mystery of salvation. For the Spirit of Christ has not refrained from using them as means of salvation which derive their efficacy from the very fullness of grace and truth entrusted to the Church."[3] This was a most notable change, and one that was greatly appreciated.

However, while recognizing at least the partial validity of other Christian denominations, Vatican II continued to assert that the one, true, holy, catholic and apostolic Church "subsists in the Catholic Church, which is governed by the successor of Peter and by the Bishops in communion with Him".[4]

Unity, then, will always need to be on Catholic terms. All roads lead to Rome. The continuing call by the Pope is to return home, and home is the Vatican. So we read from Vatican II:

> [O]ur separated brethren, whether considered
> as individuals or as Communities and Churches, are not
> blessed with that unity which Jesus Christ wished to
> bestow on all those who through Him were born again
> into one body ...[5]

Or as John Paul II put it:

> To be in communion with the Bishop of Rome is to bear
> visible witness that one is in communion with all who
> confess that same faith, with those who have confessed it
> since Pentecost, and with those who will confess it until
> the Day of the Lord shall come. That is our conviction as
> Catholics and our faithfulness to Christ forbids us to
> relinquish it.[6]

Thus, while non-Catholic Christian churches are allowed a degree of linkage to the true Church, they remain 'separated brethren'. This is a further example of what has become this book's major theme: that rather than Christ himself being the centre of unity for all true Christians, the Catholic Church inserts itself into the process. Only in communion with the true Church, the Church of Rome, can we achieve the true unity that Christ wants for us.

Most Protestants insist that Jesus meant what he said when he told his disciples that "where two or three are gathered in my name, there am I among them" (Matt 18:20). Having Christ's true presence with us as believers is not dependent upon membership of any particular organization or hierarchy, but simply upon being united with him, by faith.

I am profoundly united with other believers, not via the bishop of Rome but via Christ.

However, the most startling move of Vatican II was with respect to non-Christian religions. Since Vatican II, salvation is open not only to all Christian religions but to people from other religions, for they too reflect a ray of truth which enlightens all men.

Pope John Paul II, for example, affirmed that Muslims and Christians worship the same God. In 1985, the Pope addressed 60,000 Islamic students at Casablanca in Morocco. While recognizing the clear and significant differences between the two faiths, the Pope stated that, "We believe in the same God, the only God, the living God, the God who created the world and brings its creatures to perfection".

The Catholic Catechism states: "The plan of salvation also includes those who acknowledge the Creator, in the first place amongst whom are the Muslims; these profess to hold the faith of Abraham, and together with us they adore the one, merciful God, mankind's judge on the last day".[7]

On the one hand, it is surely right to affirm that (with the exception of Judaism) Islam is the closest of the world religions to Christianity because of its monotheism. However, the Muslim faith explicitly rejects that Christ is the eternal Son of God, that he was crucified on the cross, and that forgiveness of sins is found in his name. Islam also rejects the integrity of both the Old and New Testaments as revelations from God.

How many such contradictions need to accumulate before we are talking about a different 'God'? Or are we forced to admit that there lies within God a kind of divine paradox which results in conflicting revelations—revealing in one religion that Christ died for our sins, and then subsequently denying it in another?

Theological liberalism is clearly the source of the new-found Catholic inclusiveness. Liberalism first surfaced among Protestants in the nineteenth century and soon began to make its impact on Catholicism. By 1907, the Catholic Church was sufficiently concerned about liberalism to issue an encyclical denying its key tenets[8], and to require from 1910 that all priests swear a series of 'Oaths against Modernism' or face the consequences.

However, by the 1950s and 60s, it was clear that liberal ideas had spread widely among Catholic bishops and clergy—as seen in the excommunication of Feeney and the decisions of Vatican II. In essence, Vatican II affirmed that God's grace, which was deemed sufficient for salvation, extended not simply to other Christian religions but also to non-Christian religions. God's grace is found among all religions in various proportions with the fullest expression being found in the Church of Rome. Then, in decreasing order, the grace of God is seen among other non-Catholic churches beginning with the Orthodox churches, then Protestant denominations, other monotheistic religions such as Judaism, Islam, polytheistic faiths such as Hinduism, and so on.

Thus, far from condemning or critiquing non-Christian religions, Vatican II viewed them as implicitly Christian even if their religious life was flawed. The Council was quite clear that the 'faith experience' of a devout non-Christian can bring salvation if it is based on the desire to please God by good works as these are fostered by the conscience.[9]

Modern Catholicism has followed this logic to its conclusion and asserted that even some atheists may, through the help of God's grace, live a life that finally results in redemption. Deliberate atheism is still denounced as a sin against the first commandment, but there remains the possibility that some people could "declare themselves to be atheists on a cognitive level, yet may still be the recipients of grace at the level of being".[10] While Vatican II did not formally use Karl Rahner's expression of the "anonymous Christian", the idea was clearly present.

New Catholicism and old

At one level, there is no denying that the direction taken by Vatican II with regard to other Christian religions, and even non-Christian religions, was innovative. However, it is equally true that the views of Vatican II were the natural outworking of the traditional Catholic conception of salvation. A church which denies Christ alone, Bible alone, faith alone and grace alone is the kind of church that arrives at the Vatican II view of other religions.

This needs some explaining.

If we start with the Bible, we cannot avoid the exclusive and (to us) offensive claims of Christianity. We may plead some level of ignorance about those who cannot mentally grasp any kind of revelation due to age or profound mental disability. But for the rest, Paul is clear in Romans 1:18-32 that all have been given sufficient revelation to know:

    a. that God exists

    b. that he is powerful

c. the basic content of right and wrong

d. that those who do what is wrong deserve death.

This general revelation is available to all, even if they have never heard of Christ. And all are without excuse, says Paul, for having turned aside and exchanged the truth of God for a lie, and worshipped the creation rather than the Creator. All people everywhere suppress the truth, and worship their own idea of God rather than God's idea of himself. In effect, non-Christian religions are attempts at running away from God, not to him.

The consistent theme in the New Testament is that salvation is promised to those who have faith in Christ alone. Jesus unashamedly declared, "I am the way, and the truth, and the life. No one comes to the Father except through me" (John 14:6). If the Old Testament affirmed that there was one God (Deut 6:4), the New Testament is equally committed to the truth that there is only one way to God.

Jesus states this truth both positively and negatively. Positively, Jesus identifies himself as *the* way, *the* truth and *the* life and not *a* way, *a* truth and *a* life. And in case there is any doubt about what he means, he restates it in the negative, denying every other means of access to God: "No one comes to the Father except through me".

This clashes violently with the spirit of our age, but it is the clear teaching of the Bible. If the Bible is to be our final and determining authority, then the possibility of salvation apart from Christ is excluded. Bible alone leads to Christ alone.

But if the Bible is not accepted as the ultimate or final source of revelation—if the Church is given authority to rule on what the Bible really means, and to authorize other teachings alongside the Bible—then one can blunt the sharp and offensive claims of Christ, and find a place for other religions in God's plan of salvation. As with the developing doctrine of Mary, we can simply say that although such teaching about non-Christian religions may not be explicitly found in the Bible, the Church is able to recognize and define such beliefs in their full form as God as led her. Indeed, if we assume that God has chosen to reveal himself through the Church as well as the Bible, then it is also natural to assume that he may also have revealed himself in other churches and religions, even if in a flawed way. Bible plus some other means of revelation leads to Christ plus some other means of salvation.

What Catholicism believes about justification and salvation also leads fairly naturally to the new inclusiveness of non-Christian religions. You may recall that according to Catholicism justification is a *process* whereby a person cooperates with the grace of God to live a life that finally merits salvation. The new attitude toward non-Christian religions simply replaces cooperating with grace channelled through the sacraments to cooperating with grace channelled through one's conscience. In crude terms, sacraments are replaced by sincerity. If grace is not primarily viewed as God *for* us but God *in* us, then the 'faith experience' of non-Christians is able to produce good works in cooperation with God's grace resulting in a journey of justification.

The denial of faith alone and grace alone leads in the end to the compromising of salvation through Christ alone.

Now, none of this is to say that the Catholic Church has stopped looking for converts or preaching the gospel. The mission of the Catholic Church is still to convert people to Catholicism, for the purest expression of grace is found in the Catholic Church. The movement is one of degree not absolutes. But there is no doubt that there has been a very significant shift in the Catholic assessment of non-Catholic churches and non-Christian religions.

At one level, this changing assessment is patronizing to other religions. To tell a devout Hindu that he is a latent Christian, or a devout Muslim that he will be saved at the end thanks to the death of Christ whether he likes it or not, is paternalistic at best.

More importantly, while such a view may be in sympathy with the modern or postmodern world view, it is certainly not in sympathy with the Scriptures (as we've seen above). It is of course true that 'all truth is God's truth', and that there is a measure of truth in all religions. Islam, for example, is right in its affirmation that God is one and that he does not tolerate alternatives. The Apostle Paul himself quotes approvingly from a poem by Aratus to Zeus when preaching to the pagan Athenians.[11] But to say that it is possible to find true statements in all religions is a long way from saying that the devout followers of all religions will be rewarded with heaven. Jesus and the apostles lived in a world bursting with alternative religions, and their teaching on the matter was quite clear. There is only one way to Father, and that is through faith alone in Christ alone.

To reject these exclusive claims of Jesus because in our wisdom we regard them as unfair is nothing less than ingratitude. It was GK Chesterton, a Catholic from another era, who said, "If there are ten ways to the Father we would complain why there are not eleven, and if there are a million ways to the Father we complain why there were not a million and one."

Most of us at some level wish that salvation was more inclusive. I do! However, Jesus warns us not to be ashamed of either Christ or his words: "For whoever is ashamed of me and of my words in this adulterous and sinful generation, of him will the Son of Man also be ashamed when he comes in the glory of his Father with the holy angels" (Mark 8:38).

⊕ Notes

Chapter 2: Which Catholicism?

1. As reported by John Hooper, 'Survey exposes divide between Pope and priests', *The Guardian*, 30 January 2007.

2. "A reporter who said his wife had discovered their child would be born with Down's Syndrome [sic] and that they were preparing to terminate her pregnancy, was told: 'I swear to God: if you do it, you'll be a murderer'" (ibid.).

3. The Council of Trent (1545-63) was held to clarify and assert official Roman Catholic belief in light of the Reformation.

4. Such as the followers of the late Fr Leonard Feeney from Boston seminary. Fr Feeney took a restrictive view of the Catholic dogma *extra ecclesiam nulla salus* ('no salvation outside the Church'), and was excommunicated in 1953 for calling his archbishop a heretic and failing to appear in Rome when summoned. Fr Feeney gathered a small band of followers called the Slaves of the Immaculate Heart of Mary.

5. On 4 April 1998, Pope John Paul II received the leaders of the Italian National Service Committee of Renewal in the Holy Spirit, also known as the Catholic Charismatic Renewal. The Pope recalled that "the Catholic charismatic movement is one of the many fruits of Vatican Council II", which stimulated "an extraordinary flourishing of groups and movements especially sensitive to the Holy Spirit".

Chapter 3: Christ and the Mass

1. The 'Mass' (Latin *missa*) is probably derived from the words of dismissal which closed the Catholic church service in the Latin rite, "ite missa est".

2. Vatican II, *Presbyterorum Ordinis* (Decree on the Ministry and Life of Priests), chapter 1, paragraph 2.

3. Encyclical of Pius XII, *Mediator Dei*, 20 November 1947, paragraph 69.

4. Catholic Enquiry Centre, *Christian Ministry and Service*, The Catholic Religion: A Course of Twenty Lessons, no. 13, Catholic Enquiry Centre, Maroubra, n.d., p. 184.

5. Catholic Enquiry Centre, *The Christian Liturgy*, The Catholic Religion: A Course of Twenty Lessons, no. 9, Catholic Enquiry Centre, Maroubra, n.d., p. 129.

6. HM Carson, *Dawn or twilight? A study of contemporary Roman Catholicism*, IVP, Leicester, 1976, p. 38.

7. "And if any one affirm, that all Christians indiscriminately are priests of the New Testament, or that they are all mutually endowed with an equal spiritual power, he clearly does nothing but confound the ecclesiastical hierarchy, which is as an army set in array" (Council of Trent, session 23, chapter 4). While Catholic teaching acknowledges a limited sense in which all believers share in a kind of priesthood, it continues to insist that the hierarchical or 'outward' priesthood is of an entirely superior order: "Though they differ from one *in essence and not only in degree*, the common priesthood of the faithful and the ministerial or hierarchical priesthood are nonetheless interrelated" (Catholic Enquiry Centre, *The Christian Liturgy*, p. 129).

8. Council of Trent, session 13, chapter 5.

9. Catholic Enquiry Centre, *The Holy Communion*, The Catholic Religion: A Course of Twenty Lessons, no. 11, Catholic Enquiry Centre, Maroubra, n.d., p. 159.

10. The Roman Catholic Church categorizes the Ten Commandments differently from other churches. The prohibition not to make images and worship them is bundled with the first commandment, and the tenth commandment is separated into two commandments.

11. In fact, the only thing God allows to be in his image are living, speaking humans made in his likeness (Gen 1:26).

12. There is a ceremony found in many Catholic churches called the Benediction of the Blessed Sacrament where the consecrated host is taken out of the tabernacle and placed in a display case accompanied by flowers, candles and incense, which is then elevated and fully worshipped.

13. It was subsequently opposed by Ratramnus of Corbie.

14. John Foxe, *Foxe's Christian Martyrs of the World*, Barbour Books, New Jersey, 1989, pp. 64-65.

15. Council of Trent, session 22, chapter 2.
16. See more on purgatory in chapter 6.
17. Catholic Enquiry Centre, *The Christian Liturgy*, p. 129.
18. "At Mass we offer the sacrifice of Calvary with Christ and share in its benefits ... The sacrifice of the Mass is one and the same" (Catholic Enquiry Centre, *The Christian Liturgy*, pp. 128-131).
19. Pius XII, *Mediator Dei*, paragraph 68.
20. Catholic Enquiry Centre, *The Holy Communion*, p. 153.

Chapter 4: The Bible and the Church

1. Council of Trent, session 4.
2. *Catechism of the Catholic Church*, part 1, section 1, chapter 2, article 2, part III, 1993, paragraph 85.
3. A Catholic dogma may be presented to the faithful in one of two ways: it can be given formally, in an *ex cathedra* announcement, such as the definition of the immaculate conception; or it can be given ordinarily in the ongoing exercise of the Church's teaching office, such as the constant teaching against abortion. A dogma is a smaller subset of Catholic teaching than a doctrine. All dogmas are doctrines, but only some doctrines are dogmas.
4. "[T]hus religious submission of will and mind must be shown in a special way to the authentic teaching authority of the Roman Pontiff, even when he is not speaking ex cathedra" (Vatican II, *Lumen Gentium* [Dogmatic Constitution on the Church], chapter 3, paragraph 25).
5. So Pope Pius XII, in his encyclical *Mystici Corporis Christi* (29 June 1943, paragraph 51), stressed the unity of head and members of the body, and insisted that the body of Christ be identified with the hierarchical Roman Catholic Church. Within his encyclical he endorses Cardinal Bellarmine's view.
6. As one Catholic writer notes: "His [Christ's] permanent incarnation is the reason why believers are called in Holy Scripture the body of Christ ... the Church has thus a divine and a human aspect. These two aspects exchange properties. The divine aspect, the living Christ and His Spirit, is the infallible element in the Church, the eternally sure: yet the human aspect is infallible and sure because the divine is not present for us apart from the human" (V. Subilia, *The Problem of Catholicism*, SCM, 1964, p. 28 [footnote]).
7. Vatican II, *Lumen Gentium*, paragraph 25.
8. The Decree of the First Vatican Council in 1870, put it like this: "[I]t is a dogma divinely revealed: that the Roman Pontiff, when he speaks ex cathedra, that is, when in discharge of the office of Pastor and Doctor of all Christians by virtue of his supreme apostolic authority he defines a

doctrine regarding faith or morality to be held by the Universal church, by the divine assistance promised him in Blessed Peter is possessed of that infallibility with which the Divine redeemer willed that his Church should be endowed for defining doctrine regarding faith or morals and that therefore such definitions of the Roman pontiff are irreformable of themselves and not from the consent of the church" (session 4, chapter 4, paragraph 9).

9. Scripturally this claim rests on extremely slight foundations, via one particular reading of Matthew 16:18-19—"And I tell you, you are Peter, and on this rock I will build my church ..." Not only does the verse say nothing about infallibility, exclusive authority or even Peter's successors, but it is very likely that the 'rock' on which Jesus was going to build his church was not Peter himself, but Peter's confession of Jesus as the Christ (two verses earlier). Many of the early church fathers certainly took it this way.

10. The Catholic doctrine of purgatory states that while Christ died for our sins, we are not completely cleansed. There clings to us some of the corruption and effects of sin, and these have to be 'purged' or suffered for before one can enter heaven. This place of purging or suffering, that the soul enters after death but before attaining heaven, is called 'purgatory'.

11. The Council of Trent reaffirmed and encouraged the use of indulgences, while moving to curb the gross abuses that had come to surround indulgence selling (see session 25, chapter 21).

12. H Kung, *Infallible? An unresolved enquiry,* Continuum, New York, 1994, p. 62.

Chapter 5: The way of salvation

1. "Justification is not only the remission of sins, but also the sanctification and renewal of the interior man" (Council of Trent, session 6, chapter 7).

2. To use the language of theology, Catholicism sees sanctification as one of the grounds of justification; Protestant theology sees sanctification as following justification. Sometimes uninformed Protestants accuse Catholicism of teaching 'salvation by works' as opposed to the Protestant view of 'salvation by faith'. This is not accurate. Catholicism teaches salvation by faith *plus works*—that is, our good works and character transformation, effected by our own effort, by the work of the Spirit in us, and through the sacraments of the church, are a vital part of what saves us in the end. The Protestant view is that salvation comes through faith *alone*—that is, that our good works and character transformation through the Spirit play no part in God accepting us. He accepts us only because Christ has washed us clean. The good works are a consequence of and response to justification, not one of the grounds of justification.

3. 'Anathema' is a form of curse, usually involving excommunication from the Church. See, for example, the Council of Trent, session 6, canon 12. Likewise, canon 9 (ibid.) says: "If anyone says that the sinner is justified by faith alone, meaning thereby that no other cooperation is required for him to obtain the grace of justification, and that in no sense is it necessary for him to make preparation and be disposed by a movement of his own will: let him be anathema".

4. John Dillenberger (ed.), *Martin Luther: Selections from his writings*, Anchor Books, 1961, pp. 11-12.

Chapter 6: It's just grace

1. *Catechism of the Catholic Church*, part 3, section 1, chapter 3, article 2, part III, paragraph 2010.

2. Council of Trent, session 6, chapter 5.

3. These seven sacraments were formalized at the Councils of Lyons (1274), Florence (1439) and Trent (1547).

4. K Rahner (ed.), *The Teaching of the Catholic Church*, Mercier Press, Blackrock, 1966, p. 258. Vatican II says: "From the liturgy, therefore, and especially from the Eucharist, as from a fountain, grace is channelled to us" (*Sacrosanctum Concilium* [Constitution on the Sacred Liturgy], chapter 1, paragraph 10).

5. *Catechism of the Catholic Church*, part 2, section 1, chapter 1, article 2, part IV, paragraph 1129.

6. Catholicism makes a distinction between 'mortal sins' and 'venial sins'. Mortal sins are serious or 'grave' sins (such as transgressing one of the Ten Commandments), committed with full knowledge and consent. If a mortal sin is not confessed and forgiven, "it causes exclusion from Christ's kingdom and the eternal death of hell" (*Catechism of the Catholic Church*, part 3, section 1, chapter 1, article 8, part IV, paragraph 1861).

7. JI Packer, 'Sola Fide: The Reformed Doctrine of Justification', viewed 15 May 2007, www.the-highway.com/Justification_Packer.html.

8. The 'Hail Mary' (or 'Ave Maria') is a well-known prayer to Mary: "Hail Mary, full of grace, the Lord is with thee. Blessed art thou among women, and blessed is the fruit of thy womb, Jesus. Holy Mary, Mother of God, pray for us sinners now and at the hour of our death. Amen."

9. "All who die in God's grace and friendship, but still imperfectly purified, are indeed assured of their eternal salvation; but after death they undergo purification, so as to achieve the holiness necessary to enter the joy of heaven" (*Catechism of the Catholic Church*, part 1, section 2, chapter 3, article 12, part III, paragraph 1030).

Chapter 7: Mary

1. A Schreck, *Basics of the Faith: A Catholic Catechism*, Servant, Cincinnati, 1987, p. 280.
2. The article on 'brothers of Jesus' in the *HarperCollins Encyclopaedia of Catholicism*, for instance, acknowledges that the traditional arguments used to explain away the apparent existence of Jesus' siblings are "very thin".
3. Schreck, p. 281.
4. Peter's mother-in-law is healed by Jesus in Mark 1:30-31; the fact that he takes his believing wife with him in his apostolic travels is mentioned in 1 Corinthians 9:5.
5. Schreck, p. 282.
6. ibid., p. 262.
7. Apostolic Constitution of Pius XII, *Munificentissimus Deus* (Defining the Dogma of the Assumption), 1 November 1950, paragraph 44.
8. Schreck, p. 284.
9. These are the traditional feminine forms of the words 'mediator' and 'co-redeemer'.
10. Encyclical of John Paul II, *Redemptoris Mater* (On the Blessed Virgin Mary in the life of the Pilgrim Church), 25 March 1987, paragraph 21.
11. Apostolic Letter of John Paul II, *Salvifici Doloris*, (On the Christian Meaning of Human Suffering), 11 February 1984, paragraph 25.
12. The Rosary (from Latin *rosarium*, "rose garden") consists of a set of prayer beads and a system of set prayers. The Rosary has two aspects to it. It involves spoken prayers and meditation on the Mysteries. The prayers include sequences of reciting the Lord's Prayer followed by ten recitations of the 'Hail Mary' prayer and one recitation of 'Glory Be to the Father'; one such sequence is known as a *decade*. Up to 15 to 20 decades can be prayed.
13. Quoted in D Wells, *Revolution in Rome*, IVP, Leicester, 1972, p. 118.

Appendix: The new Catholicism

1. This is a dogma of the Roman Catholic Church. Pope Boniface VIII stated in 1302 in the papal bull, *Unam Sanctam*: "it is absolutely necessary for the salvation of every human creature to be subject to the Roman Pontiff". This was also affirmed by the Fourth Lateran Council of 1215: "One, moreover, is the universal Church of the faithful, outside of which no one at all is saved".
2. Vatican II, *Unitatis Redintegratio* (Decree on Ecumenism), chapter 1, paragraph 3.
3. Vatican II, ibid.

4. Vatican II, *Lumen Gentium*, chapter 1, paragraph 8.
5. Vatican II, *Unitatis Redintegratio*, chapter 1, paragraph 3.
6. Speaking at the Ecumenical Centre in Geneva on June 12, 1984. See World Council of Churches Central Committee Document no. 4.9.2, 9-18 July 1984.
7. *Catechism of the Catholic Church*, part 1, section 2, chapter 3, article 9, paragraph 3 (841).
8. Encyclical of Pius X, *Pascendi Dominici Gregis* (On the Doctrines of the Modernists), 8 September 1907.
9. See Vatican II, *Lumen Gentium*, chapter 2, paragraph 16; and Vatican II, *Gaudium et Spes* (Pastoral Constitution on the Church in the Modern World), part I, chapter 1, paragraph 16.
10. D Wells, *God the Evangelist: How the Holy Spirit Works to Bring Men and Women to Faith*, Eerdmans, Grand Rapids, 1987, p. 22.
11. "For we are indeed his offspring" (Acts 17:28).

Matthias Media is an independent Christian publishing company based in Sydney, Australia. To browse our online catalogue, access samples and free downloads, and find more information about our resources, visit our website:

www.matthiasmedia.com.au

How to purchase our resources

1. Through a range of outlets in various parts of the world: visit **www.matthiasmedia.com.au/international.php** for details about recommended retailers in your part of the world.

2. Direct from us over the internet:
   – in the US: www.matthiasmedia.com
   – in Australia and the rest of the world: www.matthiasmedia.com.au

3. Direct from us by phone:
   – in Australia: 1800 814 360 (Sydney: 9663 1478)
   – in the US: 1-866-407-4530
   – international: +61-2-9663-1478

4. Trade enquiries:
   – in the US: sales@matthiasmedia.com
   – in Australia and the rest of the world: sales@matthiasmedia.com.au

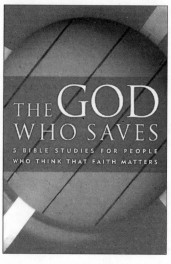